Cambridge Eler

Elements in Beckett Studies
edited by
Dirk Van Hulle
University of Oxford
Mark Nixon
University of Reading

INSUFFERABLE: BECKETT, GENDER AND SEXUALITY

Daniela Caselli
University of Manchester

CAMBRIDGE
UNIVERSITY PRESS

Shaftesbury Road, Cambridge CB2 8EA, United Kingdom

One Liberty Plaza, 20th Floor, New York, NY 10006, USA

477 Williamstown Road, Port Melbourne, VIC 3207, Australia

314–321, 3rd Floor, Plot 3, Splendor Forum, Jasola District Centre,
New Delhi – 110025, India

103 Penang Road, #05–06/07, Visioncrest Commercial, Singapore 238467

Cambridge University Press is part of Cambridge University Press & Assessment,
a department of the University of Cambridge.

We share the University's mission to contribute to society through the pursuit of
education, learning and research at the highest international levels of excellence.

www.cambridge.org
Information on this title: www.cambridge.org/9781009244770

DOI: 10.1017/9781009244763

© Daniela Caselli 2023

This publication is in copyright. Subject to statutory exception and to the provisions
of relevant collective licensing agreements, no reproduction of any part may take
place without the written permission of Cambridge University Press & Assessment.

First published 2023

A catalogue record for this publication is available from the British Library

ISBN 978-1-009-24477-0 Paperback
ISSN 2632-0746 (online)
ISSN 2632-0738 (print)

Cambridge University Press & Assessment has no responsibility for the persistence
or accuracy of URLs for external or third-party internet websites referred to in this
publication and does not guarantee that any content on such websites is, or will
remain, accurate or appropriate.

Insufferable: Beckett, Gender and Sexuality

Elements in Beckett Studies

DOI: 10.1017/9781009244763
First published online: September 2023

Daniela Caselli
University of Manchester

Author for correspondence: Daniela Caselli, daniela.caselli@manchester.ac.uk

Abstract: *Insufferable: Beckett, Gender and Sexuality* rethinks the role of gender politics in the oeuvre, demonstrates Beckett's historical importance in the development of the 'antisocial thesis' in queer theory, and shows the work's attachment to sexuality as temporarily consolatory but ultimately unbearable. The Beckett oeuvre might seem unpromising material for gender and sexuality studies, but this is exactly what makes it worth considering. This Element brings to Beckett questions that have emerged from gender, queer and trans theory, engages with the history of feminism and sexuality studies, and develops a theoretical framework able to account for what we have previously overlooked, underplayed and misinterpreted in Beckett. In the spirit of being 'on the lookout for an elsewhere', it makes a case for a queerly generative de-idealisation of Beckett as an object of critical study.

Keywords: Samuel Beckett, gender studies, queer theory, trans theory, sexual politics

© Daniela Caselli 2023

ISBNs: 9781009244770 (PB), 9781009244763 (OC)
ISSNs: 2632-0746 (online), 2632-0738 (print)

Contents

1 Introduction   1

   1.1 Insufferable   2
   1.2 Gender: Excitable Speech   6
   1.3 Sexuality: Beckett's Queer Art of Failure   9

2 Beckett, Gender, Sexual Politics   15

   2.1 The Dazzling Whiteness of an Early
       Tomfoolery: Sex Work in the Early 1930s   15
   2.2 Abortive Texts: Gender and the Politics
       of Humanism   24
   2.3 Unbearable Archives: Beckett *Amoureux*   32

3 Biting, Swallowing, and All This Stuff   39

   3.1 Sullied Images   39
   3.2 Bleached Dirt   46
   3.3 The Filthy Eye of Flesh   51

4 Conclusion   54

References   57

I toiled and moiled until I discharged or gave up trying or I was begged by her to stop.

(Beckett, 2009d, 56)

But is it true love, in the rectum? That's what bothers me sometimes.

(Beckett, 2009d, 56)

I am by no means a good translator, and my English is rusty, but I simply happen to be able still to write the queer kind of English that my queer French deserves.

(Beckett, 2011, 592)

1 Introduction

The work of Samuel Beckett, well known for its minimalism, philosophical complexity and aesthetic abstraction, might seem unpromising territory for gender and sexuality studies. But how else can we acccount for Smeraldina Rima's insatiability, manifested in her 'sexy sudorem' in *Dream of Fair to Middling Women* (1932), a novel in which the 'gehenna of sweats and fiascos and tears and an absence of all douceness' describes not only Belacqua's and Smerry's sexual encounters, but also the distinctly not 'above-bawd' experimentalism of the whole book (Beckett, 1993, 19)? Beyond an uncomfortable laughter, it is hard to know exactly how to react to *Murphy*'s Miss Carridge (to be read as one word) exhorting Celia to drink her choicest Lapsang Souchong 'before it coagulates' (1938; Beckett, 2009e, 45), or the *Whoroscope Notebook*'s esoteric Leibnizian pun on gonads – 'monads in a scrotum of circumstance'– and the 'reductio ad obscenum' of antithetical pairings in the unpublished early poem 'Tristesse Janale' (UoR MS3000, 1r; amended from Feldman, 2006, 64; Beckett, 2012, 44, 329). To move away from the slightly juvenile, misogynistic humour of the early poetry and prose, how do we deal with the discomfort caused by Lousse 'taking advantage' of Molloy (1951/5; Beckett, 2009d)? We might be tempted to think that Didi and Gogo are just making a silly joke about the potential embarrassment of having an erection when hanging themselves despite (or perhaps because of) the fact that the Lord Chamberlain thought otherwise: he requested the line to be excised from the English production of the play in 1954 (Beckett, 2011, 479–81; Beckett 2014, 83). There are castratos' screams in the thirteenth of the *Texts for Nothing* (1955/77; Beckett 2010b), an 'obscure obscene joke', echoing Mercutio's erectile jesting in *All That Fall* (1957; Beckett, 2006), Willie in his hole in *Happy Days* (1961/3; Beckett, 2006) and tin openers between 'not very elastic' buttocks in *How It Is* (1961/4; Beckett, 2014, 59–60). In 1964, naked bodies are imagined 'kissing, caressing, licking, sucking, fucking and buggering' in *All Strange Away* (Beckett, 1995, 171); in 1966, a presumed six-year-old licks the narrator's penis when told to do so (the text is called *Enough*); in *Not I*, words gush from an invisible woman's vulvar lips on the TV screen in 1975; in 1977, we are still taking part in a 'to and fro' movement, 'from impenetrable self to impenetrable unself by way of neither' (Beckett, 2010b, 167). This Element addresses these issues using feminist, queer, and trans theory, shows Beckett's relevance to contemporary debates in the fields of gender and sexuality, and argues for the need to incorporate them into Beckett studies.

1.1 Insufferable

Gender difference and sexual encounters in Beckett are sources of humour, irritation, desire, friction, discomfort, disgust, hatred, and exasperation: they are insufferable. In the pre-war years especially, the gender politics in the oeuvre are misogynistic and funny in equal measure, while any sexual relation is consistently excruciating, as the heavy-handed Freudian joke about Molloy's mother makes abundantly clear: 'my mother's images sometimes mingled with theirs [Ruth's and Lousse's], which is literally unendurable, like being crucified, I don't know why and I don't want to' (Beckett, 2009d, 58). Sexuality is also only occasionally securely heterosexual: despite Beckett's early interest in Swinburne's unfinished novel *Lesbia Brandon* (1859–68) via Mario Praz's *La carne, la morte e il diavolo* (1930), not much attention is given to female same-sex desire beyond the occasional decadent sapphic reference in the early poetry, such as 'icone bilitique' in the unpublished 'Tristesse Janale', a poem in which Charles Baudelaire, Stéphane Mallarmé, Pierre Louÿs and Max Nordau all make an appearance (Beckett, 2012, 44). A furious anality is central to *How It Is*, and male homoeroticism is often so much in front of our eyes as to have remained almost invisible, as Peter Boxall has shown (Boxall, 2004). Interpreting the figures of Lemuel and Madame Pédale in *Malone Dies*, Stéphanie Ravez found herself nodding along the Alba of *Dream*, who thought all men 'homo-sexy': 'pédale' is a derogative word for homosexual in French slang (Ravez, 2001, 137). We can't, however, dismiss the work as homophobic: heterosexual sex seems the most spectacularly fallible of all. It is also remarkably unstable: Molloy's musings, 'But is it true love, in the rectum? That's what bothers me sometimes,' tread the fine line between espousing unadventurous heterosexual assumptions about the relation between 'love' and specific sexual practices and exposing their reifying effects (Beckett, 2009d, 56).

In Beckett studies, the issue of gender has been addressed by contributions on feminism, gender, and women's studies, such as Mary Bryden's groundbreaking study (1993), Linda Ben-Zvi's work on women in Beckett's theatre (1990), Judith Roof on ungendering *The Unnamable* (2002), Anna McMullan on the female body on stage (1993; 2010), Laura Salisbury on misogyny and comedy (2012), Trish McTighe's study of gender (2019), labour and power in *Catastrophe*, Katherine Weiss' work on the 'tenacious trace' of femininity in the drama (2021), and Hannah Simpson on sexual trauma in *Not I* (2022a). When we come to sexuality, what I call its insufferable quality accounts for two representative critical reactions. On the one hand, a biographical recuperation within the 'heterosexual matrix' (Butler, 1990); this is the process, familiar to readers of Beckett criticism, that naturalises the rather disturbing role of gender and sexuality into an admiration for the author's knowingness. Alternatively, we encounter a polite glossing over anything that can be recognised as queer, as in S. E. Gontarski's well-observed but underdeveloped point about the presence of what he calls 'literary hermaphrodites' in the late prose (Gontarski, 1995, xxx). More recently, however, several studies have become more attentive to the need to account for Beckett's complex views on reproduction (Sheehan, 2006; Stewart, 2011; Salisbury, 2012), homoeroticism (Ravez, 2001; Boxall, 2004), and 'the normal' (Kennedy, 2020). With the exceptions of Leo Bersani and Calvin Thomas, queer theorists have not focused on Beckett; Eleanor Green's work on queer sexuality in the 1960s prose will change the current critical landscape (Green, 2022).

Gender and sexuality are not simply thematic concerns in the oeuvre, but formal, aesthetic, and critical preoccupations. They are also hard work. In the early prose, they make us encounter the cultural force of misogynist humour; in the middle period, they stage forms of 'abortive' textuality, as the author called it; and, throughout, they make us reflect on the place of gender and – especially from the 1960s onwards – sexuality as part of the wider question of the political in Beckett. In short, they put us on the spot.

In *Sex, or the Unbearable*, Lauren Berlant and Lee Edelman see sex as the space which enables us to understand how 'relationality is invested with hopes, expectations, and anxieties that are often *experienced* as unbearable' (Berlant and Edelman, 2014, vii). The Beckett oeuvre displays both a sustained, if sceptical, interest in any 'encounter which undoes the subject's fantasmatic sovereignty' and an awareness of the paradoxical regulatory power of any liberatory view of sexuality (Berlant and Edelman, 2014, 2). I adopt the existentialist-inflected 'unbearable' in Section 2.3, in relation to Beckett's correspondence with Pamela Mitchell, but the encounter with sexuality and gender difference is not always one that brings us into 'the anxiety-inducing arena of self-decomposure that sexual activities both beget and represent' (Wiegman, 2017, 219). It is often a comedy of misrecognition, which undoes the formal mastery needed to claim that sex has the power to undo, as is often assumed instead in the staged dialogue between Berlant and Edelman.[1] The objectless 'insufferable' of my title suggests that Beckett's texts implicate the reader in an irritable, irritating, impatient, sometimes cruel, and often comedic relation to gender and sexuality (Ngai, 2005). At times, but not always, it feels unbearable; often, it is quite fun.

This Element traces a chronological arc which follows Mary Bryden's trajectory from the 'secure deference to sexual polarities' in the early works to the gradual 'hacking away at the notion of gender', but argues, with Eleanor Green, that we have not previously noticed that the 'horribly difficult' *How It Is* marks a clear shift towards sexuality (Bryden, 1993, 14; Beckett, 2014, 252; Green, 2022, 8–37). In developing an interest in the workings of sexuality, Beckett was in step with the cultural climate of early 1960s Paris. However, his 1960s and 1970s work cannot be assimilated to the liberation movements of the time, about which he mused to Theodor Adorno in 1969: 'was there ever such rightness joined to such foolishness?' In the same letter, Beckett joked that he hadn't yet been pilloried by what he provocatively called the 'Marcusejugend', referring to the younger followers of the author of *One-Dimensional Man* (Marcuse, [1964] 2007), whom he admired (Beckett, 2016, 151). Both Herbert Marcuse and Jean-Paul Sartre expressed a keen interest in the relationship between the mechanised repetition of the 'technological universe' and its ability to 'break the innermost privacy of freedom and join sexuality and labour in one unconscious, rhythmic automatism', or as the first lesson in *How It Is* puts it in 1961, 'and that come to think of it almost mechanically at least where words involved' (Sartre, 1960, 290; Beckett, 2009b, 55).

A few years before *One-Dimensional Man*, *How It Is* turned to the 'lubricious ferocity' of sexuality as the formal and mechanical problem of violence, in the context of the Parisian 'Sade Boom' but emerging from Beckett's long-standing fascination with Sade's Dantean 'rigour of composition' (Beckett, 2009c, 117), as demonstrated by Shane Weller (2008), John Pilling (2014), Jean-Michel Rabaté (2020), Elsa Baroghel (2022), and Michael Krimper (2022); evidenced in Beckett's unpublished translations of Sade and Maurice Heine, Pierre Klossowski, Maurice Blanchot, and Georges Bataille for *transition*; and mediated by his reading of Guillaume Apollinaire, Marcel Proust, and Mario Praz (Krimper, 2022, 1–5). Neither the utopian potential of sexual liberation nor the male fantasies of omnipotence suggested by the notion of rigour fully account for Beckett's fierce economies of repetition that continued in the post-1960 period, however. *How It Is* is not 'sadism pure and simple' and does not follow a Dantean topography, although both Dante and Sade are part of the

---

[1] I owe the expression 'comedy of misrecognition' to Jackie Stacey, whom I thank.

text's digestive processes of incorporation and expulsion, which keep it alive as if it were an organism, if not quite a body.

Other works from the 1960s restage the sexual as a form of repetition, but prefer harder edges: in *Happy Days* (1961), tragicomic scenes from a marriage take place in the rather graphic landscape of mound and hole – now mutually unreachable; *Play* (1963) stages a love triangle through verbal hammering ('I can smell that bitch off you'); *All Strange Away* (1963) and *Imagination Dead Imagine* (1965) engage with the fine line dividing eroticism and pornography via painstaking geometrical arrangements of bodies. Not even in *Breath* (1966) – a farcical skit for an erotic review – does the panting stop (Beckett, 2006 and 2010b).

Despite the development from often questionable gender politics to experimental and queer sexuality, both gender difference and sexual relations remain problems which refuse to go away: the former at first a stubborn presence and, later, a source of doubt, the latter unconsoling, funny, and inevitable. From *Dream* to *Ill Seen Ill Said*, averting our gaze from gender and sexuality means missing important dimensions of Beckett's oeuvre.

The relation between Beckett's work and political issues, including gender and sexual politics, is never one of direct causality, but it is historically significant to note that Beckett's post-war experimentalism found a home with publishers such as John Calder, Jerôme Lindon at Les Éditions de Minuit, and Barney Rosset at Grove Press (Girodias' establishment turned out to be a less hospitable place), who had to deal frequently with censorship legislation when taking the risk of publishing authors ranging from the pornographic to the experimental – and often crossing that divide (Rabaté, 2020, 5–6). Sexual politics are of considerable biographical importance, too, as this Element argues by focusing on an early poem and the Pamela Mitchell correspondence as case studies. I avoid using feminist theory (or any other theory) as a critical yardstick against which to measure Beckett's allegedly wanting behaviour: as pointed out by Paul Stewart, neither regret nor condemnation will get us very far – critically or politically (Stewart, 2011). By making this choice I advocate for an approach that does not underestimate the complexity of gender and sexuality in Beckett's published and unpublished works: their much-flaunted abortive effect is queerly generative.

While not shirking away from what remains disturbing in Beckett's sexual politics, this Element is not interested in recuperating it as a value, or in 'affording storage space to the privileged seats of patriarchy', as Bryden put it (Bryden, 1993, 119). It calls for feminist, queer, and trans theory to attend to the twin dynamics of comedy and discomfort in Beckett's treatment of gender and sexuality. Feminist studies, and especially work on sexual politics, are key to analyse the prose work up to the late 1950s, the correspondence, the theatre up to the 1970s, and the early poetry, while sexuality studies are discussed primarily in relation to the post-1960 prose and drama.

1.2 Gender: Excitable Speech

Anyone interested in gender finds no shortage of evidence to back up Bryden's point that sees the early fiction as 'consistently secure in its deference to sexual polarities as discerned by a centralising male narratorial voice' (Bryden, 1993, 14). In *Dream of Fair to Middling Women*, we are offered a virtuoso display of the Smeraldina Rima's insatiable sexual appetites:

> The implacable, the insatiate, warmed up this time by her morning jerks to a sexy sudorem, she violated him after tea. When it was his express intention, made clear in a hundred and one subtle and delicate ways, to keep the whole thing pewer and above-bawd. [...] The tiffs started. [...] Still, bitched and all as the whole thing was from that sacrificial morning on, they kept it going in a kind of way, he doing his poor best to oblige her and she hers to be obliged, in a gehenna of sweats and fiascos and tears and an absence of all douceness. We confess we are so attached to our principal boy that we cannot but hope that she has since had cause to regret that first assault on his privities. Though it would scarcely occur to her, we believe, to relate the slow tawdry boggling of the entire unhappy affair, two nouns and four adjectives, to that lesion of Platonic tissue all of a frosty October morning. Yet it is always on that issue that they tended to break and did break. Looking babies in his eyes, the –, that was her game, making his amorosi sospiri sound ridiculous. (Beckett, 1993, 19)

The passage alternates between ventriloquising Belacqua – defensively reacting against Smerry's procreative obsessions – and occupying a third-person perspective, later identified as a 'we' flaunting its camaraderie towards our principal boy. Despite such an attachment, Belacqua's lack of sexual prowess and coy display of delicate sensibilities cannot escape appearing just as 'ridiculous' as his more general propensity for onanism. If free indirect discourse makes self-pleasure reverberate through the existential loneliness evoked by Giacomo Leopardi's 1829 'Le Ricordanze' (misremembered here as 'Rimembranze'), the narrator's reproduction of Smerry's voice scorns her inability to stay 'above bawd': 'I met Arschlochweh and I had to get him to finger me a bit in my Brahams', the text reports in direct speech (Beckett, 1993, 18; Caselli, 2012). Smeraldina's dubious English, which is elsewhere a cause for Belacqua's aggressive claim to intellectual superiority, is a perfect excuse not only for a cheap laugh, but also, in Bryden's terminology, for a rather secure alignment between the narrative voice and the male perspective. If you are clever enough, you can side with Bel's fragile masculinity and laugh at Smerry's monstrous appetites while marvelling at the ways in which the bawdy, now uncontained, drifts from Bel's view of Smerry to the narrator's allegedly faithful transcription of her language. The music teacher's proper name, however, makes the whole utterance preposterous in its rude take on both German compound nouns and Dickensian patronyms: any pretence at narratorial reliability is turned into a verbal game of mutual humiliation. The text cannot stay above-bawd: our mastery as readers is threatened by its own fragility, just as the mastery predicated on self-assured heterosexual roles vacillates.

In case we might be led to suspect that *Dream* is an exception, this is how the distinctively less juvenile *First Love* (1946) reads:

> One day she [Lulu] had the impudence to announce she was with child, and four or five months gone into the bargain, by me of all people! She offered me a side view of her belly. She even undressed, no doubt to prove she wasn't hiding a cushion under her skirt, and then of course for the pure pleasure of undressing. Perhaps it's just wind, I said, by way of consolation. (Beckett, 1995, 43–4)

The anti-procreative vein of *Dream* is developed into the arch sarcasm of *First Love*, in which the comedy emerges from the narrator's outraged self-assurance rather than his insecure masculinity. Wind and consolation sit uneasily next to each other, in a clash of registers that adumbrates *Molloy*'s famous *Times Literary Supplement*'s coat lining, effective because impervious to flatulence. In the eyes of *First Love*'s affronted narrator Lulu displays her impudence in announcing her pregnancy, while Molloy succumbs to the dubious charms of Circe-like Lousse:

> It was then that Lousse, taking advantage of my weakness, squatted down beside me and began to make me propositions, to which I must confess I listened, absent-mindedly, I had nothing else to do, I could do nothing else, and doubtless she had poisoned my beer with something intended to mollify me, to mollify Molloy, with the result that I was nothing more than a lump of melting wax, so to speak. (Beckett, 2009d, 45–6)

Lousse, here intent in mollifying Molloy, is accused with alliterative intensity of poisoning him in homeopathic doses with 'miserable molys', the magical drug given to Odysseus by Hermes. 'The antidote to Circe', as Beckett put in in the *Dream Notebook*, appears also in the 1931 poem 'Moly', published in *The European Caravan* in the same year under the different name 'Yoke of Liberty', in reference to Dante's *De Monarchia* and reproduced with two small variants in a letter to the editor of *The Poetry Magazine* in 1934 (Beckett, 2003, 172; Beckett, 2012, 300, 480; Beckett, 2009c, 231). 'Moly' is an eerily anachronistic decadent poem, in which the vulvar grey 'lips of her desire' part 'like a silk loop / threatening / a slight wanton wound'. Predatory femininity ('she preys wearily / on sensitive wild things') and masochistic pleasure ('proud to be torn / by the grave crouch of her beauty') come together before breaking and hanging 'in a pitiful crescent' (Beckett, 2012, 300–1). Vincent Sherry put his finger on the lingering importance of the 'the mechanical, post-natural, aftermath imaginary of literary decadence' in Beckett, but looked for it in the wrong places (Sherry, 2014, 284). Rather than in the three novels, decadence is anachronistically displayed in the 1930s poetry, where it draws attention to the threatening gulf which separates Joyce's Molly Bloom and her affirmative female sexuality (problematically voracious in its own right) from Beckett's grey and wanton predator in 'Moly': via a process of subtraction, the chasm between male modernist authors is figured as an obsolete fantasy of female anatomy.

In 1971, forty years later, *Not I* challenges the patriarchal habit of collapsing female identity into anatomy. Both the remote mouth flickering suspended above the stage and the camera close-up in the televised play in 1975, in which moving lips hypnotically become labia, hinge around the meaning of a 'godfor– ... godforsaken hole'. The hollowness of this cliché proves malleable: it refers to the anatomical origin of the 'tiny little thing', the world into which she is expelled, and the mouth on stage on which the spectators' attention is drawn, which loops back to the anatomical origin of the protagonist, and so forth. In 1997, Judith Butler engaged us in a thought experiment: 'One must imagine an impossible scene', they wrote, 'that of a body that has not yet been given social definition, a body that is, strictly speaking, not accessible to us, that nevertheless becomes accessible on the occasion of an address, a call, an interpellation that does not "discover" this body, but constitutes it fundamentally' (Butler, 1997, 5). More than two decades before Butler, *Not I* made us experience what they encouraged us to imagine. The play shows that 'by being interpellated within the terms of language [...] a certain social existence of the body first becomes possible', a point that Butler developed after Althusser and J. L. Austin and made a few years earlier in *Gender Trouble*: 'That time in court ... what had she to say for herself ... guilty or not guilty ... stand up woman ... speak up woman ... stood there standing into space ... mouth half open as usual ... waiting to be led away ... ' (Beckett, 2006, 381). As Anna McMullan has shown us, Mouth's imagined embodiment in front of a court of law, which pins her to a class-marked feminine identity ('speak up woman'), goes together with her disembodied presence on stage (McMullan, 1993). She refuses to be put in one's place by the inaudible source of interpellation: 'what?.. who?.. no!.. she!..' (Beckett, 2006, 382). To look at Mouth on stage is to look at a refusal to be defined from the outside, combined with a refusal to cohere into an 'I', whose only mention appears in the title prefaced by a negation. There is nothing straightforward about female self-affirmation in this play: initially at least, it sounds just like excitable speech. The staging of wounded femininity short-circuits the relation between language and meaning: Mouth seems to make no sense, and yet this is not nonsense. Rather, it's a shift from an idea of identity as immutable and recognisable to an attempt that involves, in Wendy Brown's words, 'not only learning to speak but to *read* "I am" this way, in motion, as temporal, as not-I' (Brown, 1993, 407). This attempt, however, is caught up in the play's repetitious loop, promising no way out.

The play stages a resentment towards the oppression generated by the posture imposed on the female actor, the potential for equating mouth and vulva, and the judgment in front of a court of law and everyday life. However, it also shows Mouth's refusal to be fixed as a female identity by a masculine gaze, as evinced by the stubborn rejection of the first-person pronoun and the stage notes, which describe the sex of the auditor as 'undeterminable'. Unstaunched, Mouth's verbal fury cuts through the pathos engendered by the spectacle of the Irish waif's destitution, in which the predatorial and charitable gaze merge uncomfortably – the latter reduced to a gesture of 'helpless compassion'. Mouth will not be mollified, not she.

1.3 Sexuality: Beckett's Queer Art of Failure

It is stimulating and perplexing in equal measure to notice how key titles in queer theory would be apt descriptions of what happens to sex in Beckett: 'Is the Rectum a Grave?', 'Sex Without Optimism', *No Future*, 'Sensual Sucking and Sociality', *The Queer Art of Failure* (Bersani, 1987; Berlant and Edelman, 2014; Edelman, 2004; Bersani, 2018; Halberstam, 2011). The frictions emerging from these connections aren't serendipitous. They take us back to the encounter between Leo Bersani – 'the inaugural voice of what is now called "the antisocial thesis" in queer theory' – and Samuel Beckett's post-1960 prose (Wiegman, 2017, 220). This aspect of queer theory is key to understand sexuality in Beckett.

Two years before the publication of *Homos* (1995), Bersani, in collaboration with visual art scholar Ulysse Dutoit, wrote of Beckett's late prose:

> And yet this resolutely narcissistic art always performs the conditions of the human subject's entry into both its natural environment and a human community. This is done, moreover, without Beckett taking into account any identifiable environments or communities. The former are often vast and lunar landscapes; the latter are the fading-in, fading-out figments of *Company, Ill Seen Ill Said*, and *Worstward Ho*, or the Hamm-like remnants of an extinct species. But it is by this very refusal to relate to – to say anything about recognizable environments that Beckett "imitates" the very activity (unlocatable

in any real space or in any real community) of a consciousness unable not to take
account of and to acknowledge itself as part of, a space in which *other* objects
and bodies inevitably appear. (Bersani and Dutoit, 1993, 90–1)

Bersani acknowledges the narcissistic quality of Beckett's prose and, rather
than judging it, places it at the centre of the aesthetics of abstraction of the post-
1960s prose: Beckett's work makes us understand, via a logic of subtraction,
what we cannot avoid doing when we think about the act of saying 'I' on the
page. Offering one of the most lucid approaches to the political in Beckett,
David Cunningham made a similar point from a cultural materialist perspective
when he showed us how abstraction, or minimalism, in Beckett cannot be
conceptualised as a style but needs to be worked for, performed as a difficult
labour of subtraction (Cunningham, 2005, 110).

In his reading of Beckett, Bersani makes identity emerge from the impossibility to be part of a space in which no other figments, objects or bodies come
into being. Beckett's double negative logic helped Bersani cast the foundations
of what will become 'the antisocial thesis' in queer theory. They shared an
impatience towards redemptive impulses: Bersani reacted against the '"redemptive reinvention of sex" that he saw at work across the Left critical spectrum'
(Wiegman, 2017, 219), while Beckett 'recognised and lamented what he tellingly termed the "redemptive perversion" at work in Peter Hall's 1955 Arts
Theatre production' of *Waiting for Godot*, by contrast to the original Théâtre de
Babylone one, which he deemed 'more like what I wanted, nastier', as Hannah
Simpson has noted (Beckett, 2011, 573, 611; Simpson, 2020, 81).

Bersani rarely made overt connections between his readings of Beckett and
his other studies on sexuality. Peter Boxall has discussed the one appearing in
'Sociality and Sexuality', and here I want to pause on the passage in *Homos* in
which Bersani compared Beckett to Genet in their invitation 'to view literature,
for example, not as epistemological and moral monuments but, possibly, as
cultural droppings'. Interpreting Beckett and Genet as part of 'a radical modernity anxious to save art from the pre-emptive operations of institutionalized
culture', Bersani argued that 'they won't let us believe that they have been
successful artists or told us some important truths. But they do, finally, let us
hear them failing or getting high on linguistic waste, and so they compel us,
perhaps in spite of themselves, to rethink what we mean and what we expect
from communication, and from community' (Bersani, 1995, 181). Bersani was
at this stage in a close dialogue with Jacques Lacan, consistently a difficult
interlocutor for Beckett scholars and yet one who is hard to ignore
(Chattopadhay, 2018; Brown, 2019). His spectre haunts both post-war Paris
and Bersani's work, as well as key theorists in his wake, such as Lee Edelman

and Lauren Berlant: the first incorporates Lacanian psychoanalysis in his work, the latter is ambivalently critical of him. Peter Buse and Rob Lapsley have argued that *Telévision* (1974), an adapted transcript of the 1973 text *Psychanalyse* broadcast by ORTF on two consecutive prime-time Saturday evening slots, 'humorously refers to "ce ratage en quoi consiste la réussite de l'acte sexuel"' – that failure in which consists the success (or completion) of the sexual act' (Buse and Lapsley, 2023, 406). Buse and Lapsley point out that for Lacan, after Freud, 'failure is a condition of the speaking subject, and it is only eliminated with the extinguishing of that subject.' This is both because psycho-analysis is a practice 'concerned with what's not working out [*ce qui ne va pas*]' and because for psychoanalysis all manners of 'quotidian errors', as Buse and Lapsley refer to anything ranging from slips of the tongue to bungled actions, 'achieve, in a roundabout and disguised way, the fulfilment of a wish' (407).

Beckett and Lacan are key interlocutors for Bersani when he was developing his 'antisocial thesis'. We should be as sceptical of this label in queer theory as much as we are of 'the theatre of the absurd' in Beckett studies: although both definitions have done a substantial amount of cultural work, they are theoretic-ally limiting insofar as they espouse the commonsensical normative logic which they apparently denounce, as if Bersani believed in the possibility of a complete denial of the social, or Beckett in the normative position which would enable us to pass a judgement on what is absurd (Juliet, 1986, 49). Previously unnoticed, however, is the historical significance of the fact that the birth of the queerly generative antisocial thesis can be found in Bersani's encounter with the bodies of Beckett's late prose – desiccated to transparency, bleached to near invisibil-ity, and muddy to the point of becoming undifferentiated matter.

Post-1960s Beckett is historically connected to the turn to queer: Bersani unapologetically rescued narcissism, once a pathologising trait defining same-sex desire, to reflect on the place of the self in late Beckett ('love demands narcissism', the narrator of chapter two of *Dream* repeats, pompously; Beckett, 1993, 39). This contributed to the contemporaneous recuperation of the slur queer, which gradually became reclaimed as a form of critical practice. The possibilities of Bersani's 'resolutely narcissistic' criticism of Beckett's late prose was soon followed by scholarly interventions such as Eve Kosofsky Sedgwick's collection *Novel Gazing* (1997), which hosted the first version of her influential essay on the dialectics between paranoid and reparative readings (the book also contains an essay on flogging in Swinburne's *Lesbia Brandon*, one of the objects of Beckett's early curiosity).

Bersani's understanding of Beckett's resistance against language's 'perverse tendency to approximate truth' make us see how the exploration of the relation between mastery and failure, repetition and boredom, generation and futurity bring together Beckett and sexuality studies (Bersani and Dutoit, 1993, 2). The antisocial thesis in queer theory originated in the primal scene of Bersani's encounter with Beckett.

1.4 Beckett, Gender and Sexuality: On the Lookout for an Elsewhere

Beckett's commitment to a perfectly balanced phrase, the musicality of his prose, the comic control of his dramatic dialogues, and the rigour of his composition pull in the opposite direction from the self-consciously performed, the improvised, and the intentionally amateurish that are often the privileged objects of queer criticism and theory (Dinshaw, 2012; Mills, 2018). Even works that have an ambivalent relation to genre and openly declare their jettisoned quality, such as *From an Abandoned Work*, are crafted meditations on the genre of the unfinished. Equally, the didacticism, irreverence, and commitment to the interrelation of art and politics frequently found in feminist literature and theory sit uneasily with Beckett's eminently non-earnest approach to politics.

The question of the relations between Beckett, gender and sexuality is, in short, a non-essentialist one: this Element does not establish a set of properties belonging to gender or sexuality studies (whose nature we could debate *ad infinitum* but whose value is established *a priori*) and then claim to locate them in the oeuvre. Conversely, it does not believe that Beckett goes beyond the assumed limitations of approaches in gender and sexuality studies. Instead, it looks at a commitment to estrange, present in both fields: if a critique of 'the normal', as argued by Seán Kennedy, is important to understand Beckett's writing and to revitalise Beckett studies, this Element does not subscribe to the exceptionalism that, in a gesture of inverted mastery, sees Beckett as able to sublate the opposition between the allegedly normal and its opposite ('how ill say its contrary?') into a consolatory 'beyond' (Beckett, 2009a, 66; Kennedy, 2020).[2]

One way to conceptualise this Element's critical approach is to focus on what Beckett called being 'on the lookout for an elsewhere'. When Beckett wrote to Cyril Lucas in 1954, 'I simply happen to be able still to write the queer kind of English that my queer French deserves,' he wasn't presciently gesturing towards queer aesthetics but reflecting on the subtly estranging effect that his bilingual (and at times multilingual) work produced through the need to be 'on the lookout for an elsewhere' (Beckett, 2011, 592). Hans Naumann, a translator and editor of French and Irish literature who, after reading *Molloy*, was

---

[2] For a compelling analysis of the different use of 'Beyond' in Freud's *Beyond the Pleasure Principle*, see Salisbury (2012, 162–9).

instrumental in having Beckett's work published in Germany, asked the author in 1954 about the influence of Proust and Kafka. Beckett replied:

> I am not trying to seem resistant to influences. I merely note that I have always been a poor reader, incurably inattentive, on the lookout for an elsewhere ['à l'affût d'un alleurs']. And I think that I can say, in no spirit of paradox, that the reading experiences which have affected me most are those that were best at sending me to that elsewhere. (Beckett, 2011, 465)

This Element asks its readers to accept being sent to an elsewhere, in no spirit of paradox. Unlike Beckett's unreliably self-deprecating statement, however, it defends the need to pay attention to aspects of the work previously overlooked. In the same letter, the author wrote, 'Je m'y suis senti chez moi, trop' [I felt at home, too much so], as a reason for refusing to continue to read Kafka's *The Castle*, prefiguring Jacques Derrida's defensive justification of his own failure to write on Beckett (Derrida, 1992, 60–1; Beckett, 2011, 462–3; Van Hulle and Nixon, 2013, 101). Derrida's resistance against what Shane Weller has called 'the threat of affinity' echoes Proust's famous line that 'a book whose hieroglyphics are not traced by us is the only book that really belongs to us', a statement that gestures towards the same need for an elsewhere, the wish for not feeling too much at home in literature which we find in the Beckett oeuvre (Weller, 2006). It is also the quotation Eve Kosofsky Sedgwick used to close her introduction to *Epistemology of the Closet*, in which she showed, after Foucault, how ignorance can itself be a form of power (Sedgwick, 1990, 63).

This Element does not invite readers to feel 'at home – too much so' with either Beckett or gender and sexuality studies. This won't result, hopefully, in an inhospitable criticism but in a renewed attention to the unfamiliar as part of Beckett's desire for an elsewhere. This critical move is not without precedents in the history of LGBT+ studies. As Carolyn Dinshaw, a medievalist, and David Halperin, a classicist, argued on the twenty-fifth anniversary of the journal they founded in 1995 – *GLQ* – the project was to offer a space for generative contestation in lesbian and gay studies, and to put pressure on the idea that we could assume a priori the kind of topics and subjects deserving investigation within this framework (Dinshaw, 2019, 6). Robyn Wiegman and Elizabeth A. Wilson's 'invitation to think queer theory without assuming a position of antinormativity from the outset' in 2015 was part of the same conversation (Wiegman and Wilson, 2015, 2). Beckett's work, often unproblematically read as part of a heterosexually normative literary tradition or diagnosed as suffering from various degrees of misogyny, provides us with a great opportunity to think about the potential of queer theory if not outside then at least beside its own commitment to a non-normative archive – 'growing sideways', to borrow the genealogical formulation Kathryn Bond Stockton used to think about 'the queer child' in twentieth-century culture (Bond Stockton, 2009). I am asking my readers to be open to the possibility of being disarmed by allowing Beckett – an author who might not be an obvious participant in queer aesthetic traditions – to be defamiliarised and to let one's archive be queered.

The risk of institutionalising the discipline of queer studies by expanding it in the direction of the canonical, if not quite the normative, goes together with the suspicion of having to absolve Beckett in the name of a contemporary sexual politics agenda. If, in the words of Lee Edelmann, the 'desire of, and for, queer theory, demands a continuous – and continuously unsettling – challenge to the institutionalization of pleasures (including the pleasures of institutionalization)', my worries here are not primarily avoiding what Lisa Duggan has called 'homonormativity', falling into the 'queer liberalism' diagnosed by David Eng, Judith Halberstam and José Muñoz, or expanding queer studies in a direction further and further away from material preoccupation with class, as Matt Brim has pointed out (Edelman in Wiegman and Wilson, 2015, 94; Duggan, 2002, 175; Eng, Halbestam and Muñoz, 2005, 1–17; Brim, 2020). My main concern is instead with resisting the hollowing out of the specifics of a theorical tradition aimed at resisting erasure, sexually and politically. Queer theory as an antifoundational discourse can too easily be decoupled from sexuality: this Element keeps firmly in place this link but resists the current push to turn 'queer' into an identity category, despite arguing that queer theory helps us see how a desire for identity runs through the late Beckett oeuvre. Conversely, it is not busy with recuperating Beckett as some improbable gender hero or sexual liberation warrior but contends that feminist theory and sexuality studies help us understand the specifically gendered and sexual dimension of Beckett's treatment of the relation between mastery and subjection, sameness and difference (Salisbury, 2012, 71).

Beckett's interest in the intimate relation between hate, disgust and desire, preoccupation with decoupling internal and external worlds, and ability to make us feel complicit in what we read cannot be fully understood without attention to gender and queer theory. This Element travels in both directions, 'to and fro': readers interested in sexuality studies and intensely fascinated by an elsewhere might not have been attracted by Beckett's outrageous misogyny, austere minimalism, and mythically forbidding density. Beckett scholars, whose monogamous commitment to the author might not have led them to situate his work within theories and histories of gender and sexuality, will be able to share with gender and queer theorists' the 'need to be ill equipped' [le besoin d'être mal armé], to use a pun of Beckett's own making

(Beckett, 2011, 462). This Element's ambition is twofold: to open the Beckett oeuvre to fellow gender and queer theorists who in the past might have been discouraged from thinking of Beckett as a potential topic for reflection and to show fellow Beckett scholars that by underestimating the epistemological value of gender and sexuality studies we have under-interpreted a good portion of the Beckett oeuvre.

This Element maps the ways which make such an encounter possible – even, perhaps, desirable. To achieve this end, I disregard the super-egoic question 'what would Beckett have thought about a book on gender and sexuality?' as part of my resistance against a familiar Beckett often imagined as either a forbidding paternal or benign avuncular figure: he could be both and yet he is reducible to neither.

2 Beckett, Gender, Sexual Politics

> Can the relationship between the sexes be viewed in a political light at all? [. . .] The term 'politics' shall refer to power-structured relationship, arrangements whereby one group of persons is controlled by another.
>
> (Millett, 1970, 23)

> Like gender, sexuality is political.
>
> (Rubin, 1984, 170)

2.1 The Dazzling Whiteness of an Early Tomfoolery: Sex Work in the Early 1930s

In 1930 Nancy Cunard, who had established her prolific but short-lived Hours Press in 1928, published *Henry-Music*. An expensively produced cloth-bound folio, the twenty-page volume was a celebration of Henry Crowder, a jazz musician and singer with whom Cunard was in a relationship at the time. Samuel Beckett, Richard Aldington, Harold Acton, Walter Lowenfels and Nancy Cunard wrote new poems or offered existing ones to be set to music by Crowder. The book cover was a photomontage by Man Ray which showed Crowder wearing a hat and a coat: visible around his shoulders were Cunard's arms, recognisable by their geometrical thinness and signature African ivory bangles, creating a black-and-white primitivist aesthetic but leaving the white heiress almost completely out of the picture.

The poem that Beckett offered for this volume was 'From the Only Poet to a Shining Whore', a title whose words were shocking at the time but now sound inevitably offensive (Beckett, 2012, 235, 31). In a letter written to Thomas MacGreevy in the summer of 1930, Beckett refers to the poem while describing an evening with Crowder and Cunard in which alcohol, music and (possibly imaginary) group sex feature prominently:

> the 14ᵗʰ was all right, because I was drunker than either Nancy or Henry. There were other people there, God knows who, but they went off early for a little coucherie I suppose, God knows also what I said & did, but I think it was all right. I was so tired at the end that I could hardly climb into a taxi. They liked the Rahab tomfoolery, God help them. Henry said several times that it was 'vey vey bootiful & vey vey fine in-deed'. He was very nice & behaved very well, and played the piano at the Cicogne, where I described arabesques of an original pattern. (Beckett, 2009c, 25)

Cunard and Crowder are defensively pitied for liking the 'Rahab tomfoolery', while an increasingly powerless God is invoked three times in the space of five lines. The silliness assigned to the poem creeps into the letter to MacGreevy by directing itself towards Crowder: the mockery, possibly aimed at Henry's American Southern accent (Crowder was from Georgia) or at his level of intoxication, produces a clownishly Black speech uttered by a subject unable to tell a joke from an aesthetic achievement. The observation that Crowder was 'very nice' and behaved 'very well' is both light on details and rooted in a racial imaginary: Crowder seems to be the only one praised for good behaviour when nobody else that drunken night seemed to have been held to those standards. If, with Toni Morrison, we see how the literature we 'revere', and not just the literature we loathe, behaves 'in its encounter with racial ideology', then we can acknowledge that there is a difficult dimension to Beckett's 1930 'Rahab tomfoolery' (Morrison, 1992, 16 and xii–xiii).

In his memoir *As Wonderful As All That? Henry Crowder's Memoir of His Affair with Nancy Cunard 1928–1935*, whose bitterly sensationalist title was not chosen by the author, Crowder recalls 'at one time meeting a young professor of languages in Paris by the name of Samuel Beckett who later went on to Dublin University to teach. Nancy became very interested in this man and he did have a very charming personality' (Crowder, 1987, 76). The memoir was heavily edited, and we should read it with caution: the words 'interested' and 'charming', for instance, are overdetermined in a text which attempts to discuss a cross-racial and cross-class open relationship while stressing the importance of dignified behaviour. One of the text's most difficult aspects is the admonishing conclusion, in which an awareness of the problems deriving from class and ethnic differences in heterosexual relations is negotiated through misogynistic disgust: 'black men are seemingly irresistibly attracted to white women', the text reads, adding that 'many black men make the most complete fools of themselves over what is practically the dregs of humanity and proudly disport themselves with nothing more than whores – as long as they are white'

(Crowder, 1987, 186). In this passage, black masculinity is endangered by a desire for white femininity, which leads to shame and ridicule. The political rejection of white superiority is crucial: Crowder expressed open admiration of W. E. B. DuBois, whose theory of 'double consciousness', developed in 1903, encapsulated the tense paradox of a self-reflective Black experience in a racist society (DuBois, 1903, 17). Monica L. Miller has described DuBois's early approach as 'justified rage and creative restraint', and Crowder's text exudes both, despite its theoretical limitations: in this section of the memoir, the analysis of the difficult interlocking of racial and sexual power relies on the patriarchal establishment of moral hierarchies among white women (Miller, 2009, 185).

'From the Only Poet to a Shining Whore' has been read as staging a dialogue between Dante – the only poet – and Rahab – the sex worker 'spared when Jericho was destroyed (*Joshua* 2:1, 21) because she helped the Israelite spies to escape from the city', as Seán Lawlor and John Pilling explain (Beckett, 2012, 304). We need to think a little more carefully, however, about Rahab's dazzling whiteness in the context of the 'young professor of languages' writing a poem for a Black singer in 1930 Paris, in a book edited and produced by Cunard. Cunard's support for Beckett's poetry (in June of the same year she had assigned the Hours Press prize to *Whoroscope*) cannot be easily detached from her radical politics and the way in which gossip about her fluid sexuality and interracial relationship were circulated for consumption in literary and aristocratic coteries.

The poem takes as its starting point Dante's *Paradiso* IX, in which Rahab is declared to be the brightest spirit in the Heaven of Venus. As Lawlor and Pilling demonstrated in their analysis of this poem and its later reworking – 'To Be Sung Aloud' – the image of Rahab's sparkling like a ray of sunshine in clear water mingles with Piccarda Donati's pearl-white brow, as encountered in *Paradiso* III, translated in the *Dream Notebook*, and mentioned in the opening of the short story 'Dante and the Lobster', which Beckett sent to Edward W. Titus for publication in *This Quarter* in 1932 (Beckett, 2012, 304–5; Pilling, 2006, 38; Beckett, 2014, 125–6). Rahab is in the company of Cunizza, Sordello's lover, and Foulquet, another troubadour, populating a canto that has often been read as diametrically opposite to *Purgatorio* XXVI, which instead inveighs against female sexual mores. Beckett expressed strong feelings against such moralism, and in a letter to Sidney Meyers in 1968 he flipped the Divine Florentine's standards into expletives: 'Turning idly pages of *Purgatory* came upon moral shit about immodest Florentine women. Was ever great poet more ballsaching?' (Beckett, 2016, 126). In *Paradiso* IX, Cunizza is unrepentant about her love for the married Sordello, Rahab triumphs as an implausibly white Christian hero, and the canto develops its unique 'rhetorical copulation', which through the use of the possessives 'mio' [my/ mine] and 'tuo' [your/s] sublimates eros through politics: "s'io m'intuassi, come tu t'inmii", or "if I could in-you myself, as you in-me yourself" (Barolini, 2014–20, *Par.* IX.81).

Possessives take centre stage in Beckett's poem too. The Italian word, both demeaning and diminutive, 'Puttanina' [little whore] is followed by the posses- sive 'mia' [my], which produces both a conjugal familiarity – echoing the famous opening of canto IX 'da poi che Carlo tuo, bella Clemenza/m'ebbe chiarito' [after your Charles, fair Clemence, had enlightened me] – and an operatic profession of love, picked up and emphasised in Crowder's arrange- ment for music, as we can hear it in the piece as sung by Allan Harris in 2006 (Barnett, 2007). The tongue-in-cheek conjugal familiarity derives from the conflation of Dante's and Joshua's Rahab, Beatrice and a sex worker: it per- forms a familiar Joycean tomfoolery that sends us back, as Lawlor and Pilling suggest, to the drunken discussion between Belacqua Shua and the Mandarin in *Dream of Fair to Middling Women*, the most Joycean of Beckett's texts, on which Beckett started to work in 1931. It follows Belacqua's renewed attack against the German word for 'female', *Weib*, which had already been used to describe the Smeraldina Rima through the post-Joycean 'coprotechnics' that characterise the novel (Beckett, 1993, 159): "'a flat, flabby, pasty, kind of a word, all breasts and buttock, bubbubbubbub, bbbacio, bbbocca, a hell of a fine word" he sneered "look at them"' (100). It would be hard to disagree with the Mandarin's own verdict on Belacqua's rant: this 'vocabulary of abuse' 'is arbitrary and literary and at times comes close to entertaining me. But it doesn't touch me' (100). The farcical onomatopoeia performed by the Italian word for kiss sends us back to Joyce's joyful, excited speaking kisses in 'Nighttown'. The word for mouth (it too is a 'hell of a word') will resurface in Beckett via the character Bocca degli Abati in Dante's *Inferno* XXXII, to whom we may want to see an early reference here (Caselli, 2005a; Beckett, 2016, 64). In the context of the disgust enabled by Belacqua's misogyny we encounter his philosophical disquisitions, à la Stephen Dedalus (complete with references to the Jesuit order) as a furious attempt to explain how 'the notion of an unqualified present – the mere "I am" – is an ideal notion. That of an incoherent present – "I am this and that" – altogether abominable':

> 'I admit Beatrice' he said kindly 'and the brothel, Beatrice after the brothel or the brothel after Beatrice, but not Beatrice in the brothel, or rather, not Beatrice and me in bed in the brothel. Do you get that?' cried Belacqua 'you old dirt, do you? Not Beatrice and me in bed in the brothel.' (Beckett, 1993, 102)

The Mandarin, amusingly, keeps failing to see what might be so wrong about what he regards as an attractive proposition: '"what's wrong" he said suddenly "may I ask, with you and Beatrice happy in the Mystic Rose at say five o'clock and happy again in No. 69 at say one minute past"' (Beckett, 1993, 102–3). Despite Belacqua's valiant efforts to keep them apart in the novel, in the poem Rahab and Beatrice tend to converge: the poet first addresses Rahab by describing her, then by invoking her through the demeaning and familiar invocation, and finally by creating an intimacy through the second-person pronoun ('You hid them happy in the high flax'). The invocation of Beatrice, both radiant and angry, is first juxtaposed to the image of Rahab ('she foul with the victory / of the bloodless fingers') and then rendered familiar 'and you, Beatrice, mother, sister, daughter, beloved'. Rather than reassuring, however, Beatrice is a 'fierce pale flame / of doubt, and God's sorrow, / and my sorrow'. The implausible 'only poet' needs these dazzling, proud, and angry women to prop him up in his imaginary Heaven of Venus.

The poem is very close in time to Beckett's first translation for what will become Cunard's *Negro Anthology* in 1934. Completed by 8 October 1931, less than a year after his poem was published in *Henry-Music*, Beckett rendered into English an essay bearing another dubious title: René Crevel's avant-guard and anti-imperialist 'Négresse du bordel' ['The Negress in the Brothel'] (Friedman, 2000, 69–73; Pilling, 2006, 33; Beckett, 2009c, 60). Cunard credits Crowder with being one of the key inspirations behind the pathbreaking *Negro Anthology*, despite his serious reservations about the expansiveness of the book and its radical criticism of the progressive project of racial uplift: the anthology pulled no punches in arguing that communism was the only possible solution to racism and the international Black question, as Cunard's foreword makes clear (Cunard, 1934, iii–iv). Her piece on the Scottsboro Nine goes as far as accusing DuBois' and the NAACP's timid diplomacy of murderous consequences (Cunard, 1934, 243–68). The book's political radicalism explains its relative neglect, which Priyamvada Gopal has interpreted as 'part of the larger elision of crucial dialectical strands in the history of anticolonialism' (Gopal, 2019, 306).

Edited by Cunard between 1931 and 1933 and published by Wishart in 1934, *Negro Anthology* included 150 contributors and was organised according to geographical areas. Covering subjects from Black history and racial politics to Black literature, music, art history and popular culture, this text has defied generic categorisations. 'Collage', 'documentary', 'anthology', and 'encyclopaedia' have all been used to describe this key contribution to Black international culture. Critics and reviewers often acknowledged that such labels were insufficient, which compounded a perceived sense of excess attributed to the editor's personality and the poignancy and abundance of material. This coexistence of lack and excess made even the left-wing publisher nervous about finding an audience: Wishart printed only 1,000 copies of the 830-page folio. If in the 1930s 'the line between the pedagogic and the political was [. . .] blurred', *Negro Anthology* framed black culture's educational and political functions within an encyclopaedic or 'total' form (Periyan, 2018, 1).

Beckett translated nineteen essays, including an anti-imperialist essay on the history of Haiti by Jenner Bastien, and Ludovic Morin Laconbe's 'A Note on Haytian Culture', an essay on the Belgian 'Negro Empire' by E. Stiers, 'Races and Nations' by Léon Pierre-Quint, an anthropological study of 'The Child in Guadeloupe' by E. Flavia-Léopold, 'Murderous Humanitarianism' by the Surrealist Group in Paris, Raymond Michelet's important essay on '"Primitive" Life and Mentality', and Robert Goffin's 'The Best Negro Jazz Orchestra' and 'Hot Jazz' (Cunard, 1934; Friedman, 2000, xxxi). Beckett dismissed his translation work for the anthology as a way to earn his bread and butter, but we need to be careful with his dismissals, especially when, as in this case, they are accompanied by a lifelong friendship with Cunard (Beckett, 2014, 442 and 153).[3] Beckett was especially harsh towards Crevel's essay, which he unflinchingly declared to be 'miserable rubbish' in a letter to MacGreevy dated 9 October 1931 in which he used a racial slur to refer to the anthology (Friedman, 2000, xii). Beckett's complex relation to surrealism has been studied by Daniel Albright (2003), Alan Friedman (2018), and Peter Fifield (2014). The latter raised the question whether the racial slur 'perhaps jars with Friedman's portrayal of a racially progressive Beckett' (Fifield, 2014, 181). While Friedman hears the language and tone 'entirely at odds with what we know of Beckett from other sources' and therefore deems the letter unreliable, Fifield claims that 'it is, in fact, entirely consistent with Beckett's language and tone', inverting the terms of the statement (Friedman, 2018, xxxiv; Fifield, 2014, 181). Since neither critic explains with sufficient precision what exactly they are comparing, we remain on equally shaky ground if our aim is reach a verdict on early Beckett's racial politics. There is something strangely reassuring, however, in trying to reach such a verdict in the first place, transforming the critic into a judge able to remain outside the difficulties that constructions of racial difference produce, then and now. Rather than sitting in judgement assuming a neutrality that far too often is implicitly white, I want to go back to Toni Morrison's point about the difficult encounter between literature and racial ideology: not unlike Beckett's letter of July of the same year, this letter

---

[3] Beckett often dismissed his translation work. He described his translations for the UNESCO *Mexican Anthology* edited by Octavio Paz as an 'alimentary job' and an 'alimentary chore' (Beckett, 2014, 153, 442).

takes down a peg or two Parisian literary life for the delectation of the Dubliner correspondent. It stages a degree of nervousness around what Saidiya Hartman and Frank Wilderson have called 'a structural prohibition (rather than merely a wilful refusal) against whites being the allies of blacks due to this [...] "species" decision between what it means to be a subject and what it means to be an object: a structural antagonism' (Hartman and Wilderson, 2003, 189–90). Hartman and Wilderson are not attached to essentialist positions, but they are determined to show us the limitations of a well-intentioned critique of racial politics, showing us instead its far-reaching structuring power. The letter bears traces of what Hartman has called elsewhere a 'political arithmetic', in which this 'structural prohibition' enables a racial slur, which had considerable weight in 1931, to trade the object for the subject's power, so that a joke enacts a form of racial violence (Hartmann, 2007, 6; Beckett, 2011, 611; Sharpe, 2016, 15).

Crevel's essay, whose title is a hyperbolic attack against 'aspermatic Baudelaire in the alcove of his official Egeria, Madame Sabatier', seems at first to be a contemporary indictment of such violence (Marder, 2016, 20). In the essay Crevel, who among the Surrealists was the most openly committed to communism, drew connections between sexual politics and imperialism. Beckett's translation reads:

> The white male takes his Mediterranean heritage, whose most fascinating characteristics were contempt for women (prostitution, civil incapacity) and a contempt for barbarism (colonisation), flavours it with a little gospel sauce and proceeds to exercise his millennial prerogatives. [...] In France Norman guile is no longer a regional phenomenon, but general. Which accounts for our national miasma of fatuous credulity as well as for that tolerance which, ever since the Valois, has encouraged an intersexual free trade in ideas and at the same time the poisonous obligation to sneer at every educated woman as a 'Précieuse' or a 'Blue Stocking'. Safely entrenched behind that fine old tradition of French gallantry, they sneer and sneer. (qtd in Friedman, 2000, 70)

A denunciation of French and European masculinity, the essay's avant-gardist language links misogyny with colonialism and rips the veil off a self-congratulatory narrative of French intellectual rationalism by pitching the mythologised 'intersexual free trade of ideas' against the well-established practice of sneering at bluestockings. His avant-garde polemic is aimed at the 'torrents of Dostoievskian colic concerning the rehabilitation of loose women' and their failure to see their own investment in the act of rescue: 'I propose to withdraw my subscription', the narrative voice defiantly asserts, 'from the Society for the Diffusion of the White Man's Morals and Physical Complaints among Savage Peoples' (qtd in Friedman, 2000, 71–2). And yet the violence that should be aimed only at the white man's imperialism and his 'demands to be entertained and debauched by [...] exotic curiosity' spills over and affects Black sex workers who are seen as the victims of capitalism, to be rescued in turn by the essay's own anti-imperialist analysis:

> now that our livid capitalism has instituted the prostitution of blacks of either sex, is as free of European squeamishness as was thirty years ago the oasis of Andre Gide's Immoralist. Then again the average Frenchman who is not interested in depravities, who is merely seeking the picturesque, can go to the brothel and meet a thoroughbred Negress. (qtd in Friedman, 2000, 173)

As a piece of cultural analysis, this passage shows how moralism cannot exempt the 'average Frenchman'. The essay's overinvestment in its own avant-gardist attack against capitalism's perverse workings, however, produces a Black feminine identity whose animalist qualities ('thoroughbred') cannot be simply ascribed to the point of view of the average Frenchman: despite its attempt at creating a critical distance, the essays' own language trades the Black woman (she's notably singular in her anonymity), turning her into 'a meeting ground of investments and privations in the national treasury of rhetorical wealth', in the words of Hortense J. Spillers (Spillers, 1987, 64). What Audre Lorde identified as Black women's simultaneous and paradoxical 'heightened visibility and invisibility' is critiqued in the provocative title of Crevel's essay, which shows how a progressive view of the history of sexual mores occludes an assessment of Black female exploitation, but amplified in its conclusion, which fails to live up to its premises (Lorde, 2019, 31; Nayak, 2014). The essay ends on a note of primitivist celebration, achieved at the cost of placing 'the naked splendor of Black peoples' chronologically and ontologically before the advent of imperialism, which remains so undefined as to resemble civilizsation tout court: 'the sordid and implacable imperialism [...] has the insolence to outrage with its ragbag the naked splendour of black peoples' (qtd in Friedman, 2000, 73). In its own theoretical collapse, the essay ends up engaging in a sort of racial violence not entirely dissimilar to the one it sets out to denounce. Its most generative aspect lies in its ability to draw a structural parallel among colonialism, sex work, and bourgeois culture, issues with which the 1930 poem and *Dream* were both struggling: 'In the Brothel: Sexual Intercourse. In the Drawing-room: Social Intercourse' (qtd in Friedman, 2000, 70; Smith and Mac, 2018, 1–86).

On 9 October 1931, the day after the *post-quem* date for his translation of Crevel's essay, Beckett visited the establishment in Railway Street run by Becky Cooper, whom Joyce had metamorphosed into Bella/Bello Cohen in 'Nighttown', to which we will return in Section 3.2. Pilling placed the two events in the same entry in his *Chronology*, encouraging a question about their relation. Without recuperating Beckett's visit under the rubric of a research trip to what *Dream* calls 'the Railway Street Academy', at this point in time the young professor is intent on revisiting 'Nighttown' and the Joycean mythology of what paying for sex can do for literature, as demonstrated by her reappearance in the invocation 'spare me good Becky' in the 1932 poem 'Sanies II'. For all its obvious patriarchal limitations, in Joyce the opposition between male erudition and female sexuality was affirmative of an exuberant Jewish (and Catholic) masculinity after decadence's commitment to misogyny. In the hands of the Protestant young professor, it can no longer be so. In the novel the Mandarin humorously berated Bel for his utter inability to experience life: *Dream* itself can be read as a painfully self-conscious performance of this inability. After the poem for Crowder about a dazzlingly white Rahab/ Beatrice ('tomfoolery') and the translation of Crevel for Cunard ('miserable rubbish'), *Dream*, via the character of Bel, gave a petulant veneer of philosophical respectability to the rejection of the very thought of 'Beatrice in the brothel' (Beckett, 1993, 137).

Beckett's discomfort with the role that misogyny played in relation to his literary young men grew in time, but in the early 1930s his work was still attached to a male modernist tradition of letting the figure of the sex worker carry out a remarkable amount of cultural labour: negotiate literary self-hatred and disgust, reflect (and at times question) the idea of male intellectual superiority, and shine with impossible whiteness against a black background. The poem, *Dream*, and the Crevel translation, however, show us that this cultural mechanism no longer worked: the dazzling Rahab, reinvented as white by Christian culture, is caricatural with her phallic 'bright dripping shaft' on the 'holy battlements'; the 'fierce pale flame / of doubt' is there for all to see in *Henry-Music*. Neither Beatrice nor Rahab can be kept in their place. Sex work and cultural work have become eerily similar: the 'Rahab tomfoolery' shows the cracks in the barrier erected to preserve white male erudition from Black female sexuality.

While translating and dismissing a Surrealist writer intent on showing the connections between 'a contempt for women (prostitution-civil incapacity) and a contempt for barbarism (colonisation)', Beckett's work stays clear of an avant-gardist anti-imperialist position – in line with its distrust of self-righteousness, scepticism towards the causal link between culture and politics and profound anti-romanticism (Friedman, 2000, 70). Beckett's own committed antifascism is evidenced in the *German Diaries* (kept in 1936–7) and in his active role in the French Resistance a few years later, and the correspondence shows considerable evidence of anti-imperialist and anti-racist sentiments, but Beckett remained distant from Cunard's activism and communism. And yet there is something politically significant in how Rahab's phallic and dazzling whiteness in the poem for *Henry Music* and the misogynist Belacqua, with his fear of flabby words, are in the early 1930s parodies of the crystalline, hard-edged modernist aesthetics celebrated by T. E. Hulme and Ezra Pound.

On 29 May 2020, in a CNN interview with Anderson Cooper, Cornel West quoted the famous line from *Worstward Ho*: 'Try again. Fail again. Fail better' (West, 2020). The quotation had been catapulted into popular culture years earlier, when it first appeared on Swiss tennis player Stan Wawrinka's muscular inner left arm, in an ornate typeface, as a sort of generalised homage to a tenacity which could be pinned onto Beckett only at a quite high political price. West did the exact opposite with those lines. He spoke of the United States as a 'failed social justice experiment', discussed the ease with which late capitalism appropriates every aspect of political struggles, questioned the wisdom of strategies such as 'Black faces in high places' by pointing out that the #Blacklivesmatter movement was forced to be born under the first Black president, and ended on the powerfully melancholic assertion that white supremacism will be with us for a very long time. At this point he quoted the Beckett line, which Cooper repeated with surprised satisfaction. It was a moment of relief to see a formidable intellectual recognise Beckett as a source of political strength after two decades of cultural appropriations intent on hollowing out the complex politics of his oeuvre (Caselli, Connor and Salisbury, 2001/2; Caselli, 2020). The exchange also generated a degree of uneasiness, however: Cooper's white face, in whose delight I saw mirrored my own, expressed the pleasure of the connoisseur, able to appreciate a beautifully turned sentence. By contrast, West repeated the line with no trace of reverence and called it, both humorously and seriously, 'the blues line from our Irish brother'; he then quickly moved on to the pressing question of how to fight against racism and neoliberalism. If Beckett's early work displayed an unre-solved discomfort with the structural antagonism of race relations, West showed that his late comedy of dispossession can offer a space to host the exhausting labour needed to oppose racism's murderous repetitiousness.

2.2 Abortive Texts: Gender and the Politics of Humanism

born of the impossible voice the unmakable being

(Beckett, 2010b, 53)

When discussing the early work, Mary Bryden wrote of the 'abortive relationship between the males and females' (Bryden, 1993, 58). In Section 1.2, I discussed how procreation was presented as a problem inescapably linked to feminine sexuality: Smerry 'looks babies' in Bel's eyes; 'Moly' anachronistically engages with decadent anxieties around predatorial femininity, Lulu's obscene pregnancy is denied; Lousse wants Molloy to work as a replacement for a dog who in turn replaced a child. While the names of these female characters wink at the glaringly made-up and the potentially bawdy, the most succinct embodiment of such preoccupations is found in *Murphy*'s eloquently named Miss Carridge.

Miscarriage and abortion are part of the dangers of feminine sexuality and the general relief at a lack of procreation that we witness in the oeuvre. They are also aesthetic preoccupations, as *Texts for Nothing*, published by Minuit as *Textes pour rien* in 1955, makes clear: composed between December 1950 and December 1951, at the tail end of a period of unprecedented creative fecundity, they stage an abortive relation to the creative process. Paul Stewart and Matthew Feldman have discussed the horror of reproduction in Beckett and his indebtedness to Otto Rank's *The Trauma of Birth*, in which Schopenhauer's vision of existence as atonement joins the trope of the 'never have been born', while Laura Salisbury has analysed *The Lost Ones* in relation to the version of Freud's death drive which Beckett encountered in Rank, 'which brings together the pleasures of intra-uterine calm and the pleasures of turning deathwards' (Feldman, 2006, 111–14; Stewart, 2011; Salisbury, 2023). In the *Texts for Nothing*, we see a transition from an abortive relation between characters of different sexes to the creation of a textual space engaged with the problem of giving birth (Sheehan, 2006; Brown, 2018). This series of texts is, even more than *L'Innomable*, the place where, in Bryden's words, a 'hacking away at the notion of gender' and 'renewed commitment to the dynamic of dispossession' take place.

Beckett described these texts as 'nothing more than "the grisly afterbirth of *L'Innomable*"' and for Paul West – an author whose literary taste always leant towards the unpalatable – they are 'an almost sardonic hymn to gestation, to the phase in which we are nothing or nobody', where the 'almost sardonic' should be read as a reference to the absence of bodies able to experience such an unsuccessful gestation (West, 1983/4, 320; Brater, 1994, 9; Sheehan, 2006, 180). In a letter to Barney Rosset in 1951, Beckett announced: 'I'll soon assemble a queer little book for Lindon, three longish short stories, the very first writing in French and of which one at least seems to me all right, and the thirteen or fourteen very short abortive texts (Textes pour Rien) that express the failure to implement the last words of L'Innomable: "il faut continuer, je vais continuer"' (Beckett, 2011, 457). The measure of the texts' success seems to lie in their ability to contradict the last sentence in *L'innomable*, to which they are linked by the repetition of the verb 'continuer'. On 12 May 1953, Beckett wrote, not entirely truthfully, to George Reavey: 'Since 1950 I have only succeeded in writing a dozen very short abortive texts in French and there's nothing whatever in sight' (Beckett, 2014, 184; see also 619; Knowlson, 1996, 397). These statements do not ask us to witness an amazing labour of love, in which the creative mind produces a text destined to live its independent life. The process provokes only a belated and grisly expulsion: the texts are failures, but they can induce something through their lateness and disregard for *L'innomable*'s injunction. They are matter to be expelled, necessarily, painfully even, but not leading to anything else, at least allegedly so, since they are peppered with references and sentences that we will encounter again in *How It Is* and *Not I*. They 'keep announcing their fatigue' and stage their failure to produce something quintessentially human, while engaging with the problem of doing just that (Cohn, 2005, 196). This harrowing process is often funny: 'Nothing human is foreign to us, once we have digested the racing news' (Beckett, 2010b, 13).

In Cohn's formulation, 'the texts cast doubt on the usual parameters of human definition – especially time, place, and memory; yet the irrepressible voice or voices remain humanly resonant, however they may lack individual subjectivity' (Cohn, 2005, 195). The difficult relations between what remains 'humanly resonant', gestation, and birth assumed a distinctly political urgency in a mid-2010s theatrical adaptation, *No's Knife*.[4] Devised and co-directed by Nicholas Johnson and Lisa Dwan, with Katherine Graham in charge of the design for the White Light Festival at New York Lincoln Centre in 2015, it was later co-directed by Lisa Dwan and Joe Murphy and performed by Dwan at the Old Vic in September and October 2016. The Old Vic performance staged gestation as an aesthetic problem by supplanting the texts' iconoclasm with theatrical images which put sexual politics in the spotlight, as recognised by reviewers. Michael Billington wrote of a staging that gave 'reckless visibility' to texts demanding an 'imagined vision of a state of non being' (Billington, 2016), while Belinda McKeon, also in the *Guardian*, delved into the relation between the personal and political:

> it's impossible, I suggest to Dwan, to encounter her adaptation and not think of the battle for abortion rights which is currently being fought in our home country. 'Of course it's political,' she says. 'But you have to give the audience the space to find their own wounds. If I'm only talking about the disenfranchised women of the world, what about the men who feel that their identities are curtailed? What about the immigrants who don't feel welcome in this country?' (McKeon, 2016)

For Dwan, according to the interview, 'the danger about overtly politicising Beckett is that you ruin all the connotations that other people might draw from

---

[4] The production is unrelated to the 1975 short prose collection with which it shares its title (Beckett, 1975).

him. He made these wounds universal.' In response to McKeon's link with the contemporary protest to repeal the eighth amendment in Ireland, Dwan rejected a narrow definition of political Beckett in favour of something roomier, but also looser. Through a process of expansion, the 'wound' of no's knife became universal: if Beckett is a political author, the politics of his oeuvre can be linked to a specific cause only at the price of losing something. This is a well-rehearsed debate in Beckett studies: it is based on the opposition between politics as something local, recognisable, linked to action – if perhaps not necessarily activism – and a more universal recognition of human suffering, inherently but not specifically political. Through a comparative analysis of *Catastrophe*, the *Texts for Nothing*, and *No's Knife*, this section uses feminist and gender theory to achieve two aims: explain how the Beckett oeuvre's remains reluctant to be recruited to a specific political agenda while displaying an ability to dissect power relations, and delineate the limitations of the idea of universal humanism to account for such a dynamic.

Catastrophe was one of Beckett's most overtly political plays: dedicated to Vaclav Havel, it was written at the request of the Association Internationale de Défense des Artistes and staged at the Avignon Festival in the summer of 1982, in a production vehemently disliked by Beckett himself. As recognised by Trish McTighe, the relation between power, labour and gender is central to the play (McTighe, 2019). The role of 'The Assistant', the female figure equipped with a notepad, seems at first to be based on her blandness: the stage directions claim that her 'age and physique' are 'unimportant'. By doing so, however, they draw attention to the fact that the assistant's gender is sufficient to call for such a description, even when we are denied one. She assists the director in putting on the finishing touches to the performance of torture ('I make a note,' she repeats), which eventually gains the wretched victim a 'distant storm of applause'. She takes instructions while the director scathingly rejects all her suggestions. Within the context of a performance of torture, the female assistant is shouted down and instructed to implement changes made by the cigar-smoking director to gain maximum effect. She is, however, not a victim but a perpetrator: when propping up power, femininity facilitates and participates, but is as unimportant as the Assistant's age and physique. Borrowing from phenomenology, we can say that the Assistant is a 'Being-for-the-gaze' only, never a 'Being-for-thinking' (Maude and Feldman, 2009). Even though the play shows her struggling to be the latter when she helpfully suggests how the arranged victim would 'look better', this act is what confines her to the former. *Catastrophe* does not condone her role, but stages it angrily, making us deeply uncomfortable in the process: Stephen Thomson has argued that this effect in Beckett's late drama is achieved through a critical rather than allegorical relationship with phenomenology – 'dedicated not to exemplifying or explaining but to delivering an experience that puts us on the spot' (Thomson, 2010, 79).

Catastrophe's Assistant can make us reflect on the difficulties faced by a woman actor and co-director when reclaiming the *Texts for Nothing*. Dwan encouraged us to look for the universal wound that the production staged, rather than individual wounds, or to recognise our individual wounds as part of much deeper, universal ones. And yet, universality has never worked well for those excluded from its definition – the gendered category 'woman' being one of them. As Simone de Beauvoir put it in her classic formulation from the mid-1940s: 'Certainly woman like man is a human being; but such an assertion is abstract.' She continued:

> the relation of the two sexes is not that of two electrical poles: the man represents both the positive and the neuter to such an extent that in French *hommes* designates human beings, the particular meaning of the word *vir* being assimilated into the general meaning of the word 'homo'. Woman is the negative, to such a point that any determination is imputed to her as a limitation, without reciprocity. (de Beauvoir, 1949, 5)

Despite the changes which occurred in the late twentieth and early twenty-first centuries in the use of the term 'man' as a universal, de Beauvoir is still useful to think about how a body on stage recognisable as female makes us rethink the politics of universal humanism which *No's Knife* espouses.

Louis Althusser saw 'the problematic of universal human nature' as one of 'transparency itself'. In *Marxism and Humanism* (1964) he wrote:

> If the essence of man is to be a universal attribute, it is essential that concrete subjects exist as absolute givens; this implies an empiricism of the subject. If these empirical individuals are to be men, it is essential that each carried in himself the whole human essence, if not in fact, at least in principle; this implies an idealism of the essence. This relation can be inverted into its 'opposite' – empiricism of the concept/idealism of the subject. But the inversion respects the basic structure of the problematic, which remains fixed. (Althusser, 1964)

For Althusser, late Marx's great 'scientific discovery' was the rejection of the 'essence of man' as a theoretical presupposition and its recognition as an ideology, replacing the 'old couple individual/human essence' with a 'historico-dialectical materialism of *praxis*'. Late Marx, in Althusser's view, developed his 'theoretical anti-humanism' as a rejection of humanism's theoretical status while 'recognizing its practical function as an ideology'. Althusser reread late Marx via psychoanalysis to open a dialectical space where we can see the usually transparent relationship between humanism as a universal essence and an unacknowledged empiricism of the subject: universal humanity (the essence of man) is based on forgetting the mutual dependency between empirical subject and universal essence. If we enrich Althusser's point with de Beauvoir's thoughts on gender, we can see that the illusion of 'the essence of man as a universal attribute' is easily kept alive when the body on stage is recognised as male, standing for the whole of humanity, but it becomes quite hard to keep up when what the feminine state of exception is under the spotlight. In Billington's symptomatic words, we have 'reckless visibility' where there should be 'strange, metaphysical texts' (Billington, 2016).

No's Knife showed how a subject recognisable as female on stage stops propping up the link between masculine subjectivity and universal essence. Suddenly, to look at her was no longer to look, transparently, at universal humanity but to look at femininity: the universal was turned into a specific message – the adaptation of these abortive texts must be about abortion rights. Femininity broke the transparent illusion of 'the essence of man' but was soon confined to work only as an ideology formation invested in a particular cause, something that Dwan resisted by refuting a biographical or a nation-based interpretation and vindicating a universal quality for the wound of no's knife. Femininity worked as both dramatic opportunity and limitation.

The *Texts for Nothing* speak to the problem of a shared universal humanity by producing a space in which a voice fails to bring a self or another into life: 'No voice ever but it in my life, it says, if speaking of me one can speak of life, and it can, it still can, or if not of life, there it dies, if this, if that, if speaking of me, there it dies, but who can the greater can the less': the *Texts for Nothing* never claim to create a life, despite being constantly busy with its existence and its extinction (Beckett, 2010b, 51). They make us participate in a long labour that leaves us with no product, although the very convulsions of the texts inevitably generate something that sounds a little human (Cohn, 2005, 202).

On stage, however, although the voices performed an incoherent, even disorganised subjectivity, we knew exactly where we stood in relation to the feminine body, which was there for us to look at, wearing a slip, dark tights looking bloodied, alluding to a bodily wound: we could not forget about it. Stuck in a vaginal crack in the earth, moving quite freely on stage, sitting on a swing, Dwan embodied the struggle in which femininity needs to engage to reach beyond the strict confines of roles such as the Assistant. On stage in 2016, the image of femininity made itself available as a firm identity, pushing against the restrictive expectations attached to a gendered 'physique' usually far from 'unimportant' and defiantly asking us to identify her as universal, standing for the 'essence of man'.

In Beckett's plays the female body is rarely directly accessible: ghostly and in tatters in *Rockaby* and *Footfalls*, halfway visible – in a bin in *Endgame*, a mound of earth in *Happy Days*, and an urn in *Play* – and reduced to a synecdoche in *Not I*. We need to work hard to consume the image of a female body without realising we are doing so. In the adaptation of 'Text for Nothing 5', in which femininity was 'on trial', to borrow from McMullan's happy formulation, the audience was asked 'to be judge and party, witness and advocate', to look at ourselves performing those roles: unlike the rest of the production, this moment implicated us (and itself) in the less than pure pleasure of looking. For the most part, however, the staging encouraged us to enjoy consuming the body on stage as a traditional figuration of femininity, without asking our perception to founder or our 'pleasure in looking' to tip 'over into the register of excess' in ways analogous to what the *Texts for Nothing* do on the page, where the relationship between the 'I' and the 'you' is one of fracture, partial identification, pleasure, and distrust (Rose, 1986, 227). This partial identification includes the question of gender identity, which vacillates precisely when addressing the problem of generating something 'human in kind', as in 'Text for Nothing 13':

> The faint hope of a faint being after all, human in kind, tears in its eyes before they've had time to open, no, no more stopping and wondering, about that or anything else, nothing will stop it any more, in its fall, or in its rise, perhaps it will end in a castrato scream. (Beckett, 2010b, 52)

The passage estranges the human ('human in kind'), while the voice (it) and the faint being (it) become difficult to tell apart, so that 'in its fall, or in its rise' can be read as a trajectory of this being and as the voice's falling and rising not only in volume but also pitch. The hypothesis that it will end in a castrato scream brings together this oscillating voice, whose refined, estranging musicality becomes a 'scream', and the being who, despite its faint humanity (tentatively signified by a newborn's tears) is not securely anchored to gender (Gavin, 2022, 99–100, 105). As Rose argued, 'if meaning oscillates when a castrato comes onto the scene, our sense must be that it is in the normal image of the man that our certainties are invested and, by implication, in that of the woman that they constantly threaten to collapse' (Rose, 1986, 232).

The rise and fall of the voice/being questions the link between being and gender in a way that addresses the ideological links between masculinity and the universal 'essence of man' and femininity and gestation. The feminine pronoun 'elle' in the French version is translated into English as 'it', constructing 'elle' as a grammatical necessity rather than an essentialist assumption. Indeed, when in 'Text for Nothing 13' associations to the maternal surface, they are defamiliarised by a logic of Nietzschean resentment: 'I wouldn't pity it if it had made me, I'd curse it, or bless it, it would be in my mouth, cursing, blessing, whom, what, it wouldn't be able to say, in my mouth it wouldn't have much to say, that had so much to say in vain' (Beckett 2010b, 52). In the words of Eve Kosofsky Sedgwick: "'Good", Nietzsche remarks, but his affect here may be rather enigmatic, 'is no longer good when your neighbour takes it into his mouth'" (Sedgwick, 1990, 157; Nietzsche, 1886, 53).

The 2016 staging offered us a less troubling image of femininity. Tellingly, the show was labeled 'lyrical' and 'mesmerising' by reviewers, in a silent acknowledgement of the production's investment in the perfection of a theatrical image which in its aesthetically acclaimed form serves to maintain a stable form of sexual recognition (Rose, 1986, 232). *No's Knife* evened out what in the *Texts for Nothing* was the fraught relationship between aesthetics, politics, and sexual politics: a voice which is feminine in the French text but neutral in the English attempted to generate something a little human but ended up with 'infant languors in the end sheet' (Beckett, 2010b, 52), questioning the 'purity' of generation (including creative generation) and producing 'the unmakeable being' 'born of the impossible voice' through an undecidable castrato scream closing a set of texts described by the author as a 'grisly afterbirth'. If there is a residual humanism at work on the page, it is one disanchored from a secure attachment to male universalism. It questions the connections between gender, gestation and parturition that affect traditional associations with female body and male mind.

No's Knife was compelling in its ability to remind us, through its staging of a gendered body, of the difficulties we encounter when we think of Beckett in relation to the politics of a humanism conceptualised as universal. Once femininity and sexuality entered the field of vision, the reassuring ability to witness yourself as simply human crumbled, bringing down with it the unacknowledged relation between the empiricism of the subject and the idealism of the essence. While the stage adaptation partially addressed the relation between universal humanism and gender politics, the *Texts for Nothing*, and especially 'Text for Nothing 13', asked us to reflect on what we are called to see: 'there can be no work on the image, no challenge to its powers of illusion and address, which does not simultaneously challenge the fact of sexual difference' (Rose, 1986, 226). Rather than settling on a generalised universal wound or a specific ideological formation, every 'mute micromillisyllable' in the *Texts for Nothing* keep us wondering about the far from obvious relationship between generation, parturition and creativity. The times might be ripe for an adaptation in which assumptions between gender identity, generation, and something 'human in kind' can be questioned on stage.

2.3 Unbearable Archives: Beckett *Amoureux*

Suzanne found the faces excessively made up and characterized: aging missus and exciting mistress, etc. This would be completely wrong. They are all in the same dinghy at last and should be as little differentiated as possible. Three grey disks.

(Beckett, 2014, 584)

I dislike the ventilation of private documents. These throw no light on my work.

(Beckett, 2014, 92)

Unbearable.

(Beckett, 2009a, 77)

This section gravitates towards the biographical to interrogate archival material which has proven resistant to critical incorporation. My case study is Pamela Mitchell's correspondence with Samuel Beckett, donated in 2002 to the Beckett International Foundation at the University of Reading by Mitchell's estate (Gussow, 1997). Over a period of seventeen years, Beckett wrote sixty-one letters to Mitchell, now catalogued as MS 5060. Moving from intimacy to polite distance, these letters trace a trajectory from an intense, short-lived relationship in Paris to courteous occasional exchanges across the Atlantic. When Beckett travelled to New York City in 1964 they met once more. Mitchell described 'this later friendship' to James Knowlson as an 'amitié amoureuse' (qtd in Knowlson, 1996, 404).

The letters started in September 1953, shortly after Becket met Mitchell in Paris, where as an associate of Barney Rosset she was sent to negotiate a deal for the English rights to *Godot*. The correspondence continued until the 1970s, although the intense traffic slowed down considerably after 1956, the year in which Beckett met Barbara Bray, with whom he was in a relationship 'that was to last, in parallel with that with Suzanne [Déchevaux-Dumesnil], for the rest of his life' (Knowlson, 1996, 459). Nineteen letters, including a number of truncated ones, have been published in the second volume of the correspondence, but when read in its entirety the very personal exchange between Beckett and Mitchell makes for uncomfortable reading: it is hard to know what to make of such intimacy if not echoing Mitchell's own sense that such a combination of intensity and longing cannot do anyone much good (Mitchell, 7 June 1954, UoR MS5060/54; Walker, 2020, 129).

Knowlson has addressed the difficulty of dealing with this 'terrible intensity' by interpreting Beckett's letters in the context of his grief about his brother, with whom he spent the five months preceding his death in September 1954 (Knowlson, 1996, 398–404). Ascribing the peculiar flatness of many of the letters to grief is a sensitive and historically unexceptionable gesture, but it does not fully address the problem of what to do with these letters from a critical point of view. Perhaps, unlike Knowlson, we should simply politely ignore the existence of the whole correspondence and rely exclusively on the published selection. Many have done just so with the result, as John Pilling put it in his astute if unforgiving review of *LSB2*, to have Mitchell appear 'little more than a shoulder to cry on and a few weeks of romance to be remembered' (Pilling, 2012, 112). Pilling argued that with the excision of many of the Mitchell letters we lost the rich testimony of Beckett's feelings not just for Mitchell but also for his brother during his long and difficult stay in Ireland. Pilling is joined by several other reviewers in lamenting the omission of so many letters in this correspondence from the second volume of the published letters. In 2011, for instance, Glyn Vincent wrote: 'But this rich material that might otherwise provide for the warp and weave, the texture of Beckett's life just when it is most needed, is deemed less significant than notes about contracts, option rights, possible productions, and even memos to printers about punctuation.' By opposing rich material to threadbare pedantry Vincent put down these 'puzzling gaps' to a 'prickly reserve about discussing certain aspects of Beckett's personal life' (Vincent, 2011).

The dispute about what counts as life, in which intense affectivity is set against memos about punctuation, does not overcome the intractable obstacle of Beckett's own wishes. In a letter to Martha Fehsenfeld on 18 March 1985, reproduced – perhaps slightly defensively – in the first volume of the letters, Beckett wrote:

> I do have confidence in you & know that I can rely on you to edit my correspondence in the sense agreed with Barney [Rosset], i.e. its reduction to those passages only having bearing on my work. It would be a most difficult job and I am relieved at the thought of its being in such devoted and capable hands as yours. (Beckett, 2009c, xiv)

As it is often the case with correspondences, the case rests on who owns the facts of their own life, including the distinction between affect and punctuation (Rose, 1991, 65). Beckett's impossible wishes leave us with the question that Pilling rightly asks: 'who, or what, is being protected here, or (in the classic formulation) *quis custodies custodiet*?' (Pilling, 2012, 21). Unlike Vincent, I am unconvinced that prudishness guided the expurgation of the Mitchell letters; many Beckett critics have revelled in Beckett's magnetism, as the frequent mention of Barbara Bray's *coup de foudre* attests. It might be plausible to blame the omission on an excess of caution in following Beckett's stated wishes: Dan Gunn's unconvincing claim that the inclusion of the Mitchell letters in the volume he co-edited 'would not have radically altered our perception of

Beckett, the man or the writer' lends itself to be read in this light (qtd in Tranter, 2013). Roy Foster described the letters as 'passionate and self-lacerating', but they are also unexceptionable because they produce a strange familiarity: these letters could have been written by anyone vacillatingly in love.

The mixture of impersonal language of affect and intense intimacy makes for unnerving reading, calling on scholars to defend the relationship to avoid falling into moralistic or voyeuristic positions. Describing Mitchell's decision to move to Paris, for instance, Knowlson wrote that it 'made things far more difficult for him [Beckett], since he was still living in a fairly small apartment with Suzanne and it was not easy to keep his meetings with the young American woman secret', before adding 'perhaps he did not even try' (Knowlson, 1996, 400). While interested in neither character assassination nor stating that Beckett was only human after all, I want to attend to the unbearable quality of these letters: they are hard to read not because they reveal the 'rich texture of Beckett's life', but because they offer us an unusually intimate but also a rather banal Beckett – an un-Beckettian Beckett. Although on occasion the correspondence reads like something out of Beckett, it more often displays a curious clichéd and impersonal quality, which produces an interesting critical block: the way in which tenderness and distance take shape in a language so familiar as to almost grate seems to leave little space for anything other than a gesture of helpless compassion. These letters are a good case study to develop approaches to what Gontarski has called the 'grey canon', able to account not just for the moments of continuity between published and unpublished material (in which the language of intimacy and literary language coincide) but also those in which a recognisable Beckettian complexity is replaced by a rather banal lover's discourse (Gontarski, 2006, 143; Barthes, 1977). This correspondence ultimately helps us de-idealise the notion of authority which shapes Beckett studies and highlights the difficulties which we encounter when we try to incorporate, rather than justify or expel, aspects of the complex picture of the correspondents.

Some letters, as Knowlson demonstrated, are memorably literary: 'And so soon it will have been another day and all the secret things inside a little worse than they were and nothing much been noticed' (undated, probably mid-June 1954; Beckett qtd in Knowlson, 1996, 402). The future anterior is figured as repetition, the 'impossible heap' of time accumulates, there is no firm source of agency, and, as John Pilling notes, we encounter again the phrase 'secret things', which is a line adapted from Dante's *Inferno* III, line 21 ['le secrete cose'], which also appeared in line 4 of the 1931 poem 'Enueg I' and in the letter to Higgins quoted in Section 3.2. Here, the time of grief becomes eminently Beckettian: never securely anchored in the category of the past, the future is conceived as both impending and repetitious, decaying almost imperceptibly. This is how time behaves in *Endgame*, as noted by Knowlson and Pilling, and it comes as no surprise that critics advocating for this correspondence to be published argue for the literary relevance of these letters: the 'secret things' are both figured as intimate (what has not been discussed about his brother's illness) and familiar – the repetition of a line translated from Dante's *Inferno* performs the secretiveness of the secret things. Here, the grey canon poses very similar problems about echoes and repetitions to those encountered in the published oeuvre: certain lines, phrases, and words migrate across and traverse the published and unpublished work, turning the correspondence into an archive of memories, breaking down the opposition between affect and marks on the page.

Against this example of Beckett's literary, complex and moving prose, we encounter considerably different constructions of time and subjectivity. About a month before his brother's death, Beckett writes: 'I'm very tired this evening and can't do much for us. Soon the leaves will be turning, it'll be winter before I'm home. And then? It'll have to be very easy whatever it is, I can't face any more difficulties, and I can't bear the thought of giving any more pain, make what sense you can of that, it's all old age and weakness, why will you not believe me? (6 August 1954, UoR MS5060/35; Knowlson, 1996, 403; Beckett, 2011, 493). Knowlson reads this letter as a clear message: 'the sadness of his brother's illness and death had sharpened him to the distress caused by deceit and emotional infidelity and he had witnessed far too much pain to be willing to inflict any more'. Beckett, he writes 'was in no doubt from her letters that Pamela was very much in love with him. But the affair could not be allowed to continue. So, at the end of November, he took the decisive step to "call it a day", arguing that, although he was very fond of her, he did not love anyone' (Knowlson, 1996, 403). Knowlson at first shelters Beckett from his own decision to break up with Mitchell through a passive construction but quickly re-establishes Beckett's agency by qualifying it as a 'decisive step' – perhaps even overwhelmingly so, since it needs to be followed by Beckett's own euphemism. The uncomfortable position of the critic is that of attempting to side with Beckett while implicitly recognising Mitchell as the victim. The letter's opening is considerably blunter, using the first-person plural and the imperative 'shall' before the injunction to 'call it a day' and the first person singular when claiming to be unable to love anybody. It continues:

> For me things must go on as they are. I have not enough life left in me even to want to change them. They may change and leave me alone. I shall do nothing to try and stop them either. The notion of happiness has no meaning at all for me any more. All I want is to be in the silence . . .

> Don't imagine I don't feel your unhappiness. I think of it every hour, with misery. For God's sake admit to yourself you know nothing of me and try and believe me when I tell you what I am. It is the only thing will help you. You will be happy one day and thank me for not involving you any deeper in my horrors. (Beckett, UoR MS5060/43; qtd in Knowlson, 1996, 403)

The phrase 'All I want is to be in the silence … ' is both fatigued and self-assertive: a secure act of renunciation that denies its paradoxical status. Vincent read this as lyricism, a description that does not help us to come to terms with the aggression of the second part of this letter: an exasperated invocation of God is followed by an 'I' that claims to know what is best for the 'you'. This 'I' knows what he is, tells her, and demands that she 'believes' him: this, apparently will be the cure – 'the only thing will help you'. The use of 'to be fond' as a signal of profound ambivalence can be traced back to other letters, as shown in a letter written as early as 5 October 1953, in which Beckett encourages Mitchell to be fond of him, but not too much so, while claiming not to be worthy of her love and bound to make her unhappy, before gently rebuking her for not having asked him for the money she would have needed to stay on in Paris (Beckett, UoR MS5060/02). In one unsigned letter dated 14 October 1953 (probably a draft or a copy), Mitchell responds by writing, 'I have never had a vacation from which it's been so hard to recover and what's worse am not at all sure I want to.' She continued:

> Despite all distractions however I find myself thinking of you most of the time and I gather considerably more than you suggest I should. Was a little frightened after I'd mailed my letter at my courage in having written it. But meant what I said and as for being 'fond but not too fond' just cannot manage it, though met you so briefly and never before susceptible to so brief an encounter with anyone. Wish I had stayed for a bit. If you really have horns and a tail, embezzle or beat up women who love you or whatever it is at which you so darkly hint maybe I'd have discovered it and be deterred. Or might just have been more fascinated. As it is here I am emoting all over the place with no decent sense of reticence or proper womanly modesty and I'm afraid embarrassing you, [words erased] though I hope not. Anyway miss Paris dreadfully and miss you more than I have any intention of telling you at the moment. Hope you had a good rest and a good time in the country and feel fine again. Your doctor obviously has not soul. But please don't crever. Love, [not signed]. (Mitchell, UoR MS5060/03)

Few of us could bear the horror of having our correspondence to a former lover dissected, and my intention here is not to hold Beckett to a moral standard set up so high that he can only fall short of it. A refusal to turn morality into 'a form of licensed pleasure' does not exempt us, however, from having to recognise that reading these letters as exclusively about the author's mourning or interpreting them as an expression of lyricism means wishing away their and our own ambivalence (Rose, 1991, 8, 6, 74). Beckett, an author much loved for his restraint, his ability to consistently be on the right side of history, and his generosity, is here making a melancholic spectacle of himself. I do not mean this in moralistic terms but literally: as a letter written on 12 January 1954 put it: 'Yes I'm gloomy, but I always am. That's one of the numerous reasons you shouldn't have anything to do with me. More than gloomy, melancholy mad' (Beckett, 2011, 443). Unlike Hamm's 'can there be misery loftier than mine?', in which 'the full broken energy of Beckett's comedy' undercuts the insufferable self-pity, the letter does not work through it (Piette, 2011, 282).

The critic may want to wish away her own ambivalence towards such a spectacle: the letters are not morally reproachable, but very hard to read because they are so predictable (we have all been there: 'it's not you, it's me'). Claiming to be able to tell and predict the truth ('you will be happy one day and thank me'), these letters bring together sexual and literary proximity in ways that are certainly not reassuring. Knowlson recognised such an ambivalence:

> His letters after her departure are loving and tender: 'Wish I could get up now and got o 4 bis [rue de la Grande Chaumière] and lie down and never get up again. We'd play square words, between times, and every six hours you'd spoonfeed me with a hamburger and the pianist would die. No? Yes? You're right.'
> It is as if, given the safety of the distance, he wants to restore, even reclaim their intimacy. (Knowlson, 1996, 404; 26 March 1955, UoR MS5060/54; Beckett, 2011, 532)

The mock (self-)dialogue 'No? Yes? You're right' makes clear that this fantasy of passivity – never getting out of bed, playing with words, being regularly spoonfed hamburgers – needs to be brought to an end. Such an ending is, however, placed in Mitchell's hands ('You're right'). Although the letter quoted by Beckett is dated 1955, the pattern repeats what we see at play from the very first archived letter: 'Those were good evenings we had, for me, eating and drinking and drifting through the old streets. That's the way to do business. I'll often be thinking of them, that is of you' (26 September 1953; Beckett, 2011, 406). And again, in January 1954: 'Ate canard à l'orange at the Îles Marquises, under the trout aquarium. Why don't you take up quarters at the Montalembert? / Love and succedanea / Sam' (12 January 1954; Beckett, 2011, 444). Temporal and spatial distance are central to how this correspondence keeps love and loss alive. Ambivalence marks the history of this correspondence, too: Mitchell kept it and eventually made it public, thus running the risk of being read either as a victim or wanting to reclaim privileged access to

Beckett. Such interplay of loss and ambivalence explains why it is proving so hard to contain these letters in the critical discourse.

One way in which critics have attempted to do this has been by reading Pam in *How It Is* as figuring Mitchell. Dominic Walker's reaction against the previous marginalisation of the correspondence is a useful strategy to argue for the historical particularity of the text, despite failing to assuage my reservations about the vast critical leap he needs to make to argue for the text's normalisation of 'political sexual violence and normative romantic sadism' (Walker, 2020, 119; Beckett, 2011, 492). While Walker's thesis fits my periodisation, which sees sexuality becoming in *How It Is* a central formal preoccupation, it fails to account for the text's refusal to have a content, politically laudable or otherwise. If 'Pam' is there, she is part of the process of digestion and expulsion which makes *How It Is* not 'about' something, as Barbara Bray put it in her review presented on the BBC Third Programme on 2 February 1961. Beckett liked the review 'very much – quite sincerely' and perhaps not without a dose of healthy narcissism. He wrote to her the next day: 'You have "understood" the book as no one so far. [...] What you say of its being not about something, but something, is exactly what I wrote of <u>Finnegans</u> in the <u>Exagmination</u>' (3 February 1962; Beckett, 2014, 397). If we wanted to read Pam as a way of incorporating Mitchell into the oeuvre and expelling her from it – according to the peristaltic logic of the text which I will discuss in Section 3.1 – we would need to develop a more robust feminist framework, able to account, for instance, for the fact that the preposterous 'Pam Prim' appears as 'the wife' ominously rhyming with a 'life' soon to be lost (Salisbury, 2016 and 2012). Perhaps one way forward might emerge from Pilling's observation about the increasingly important role of female correspondents from 1953 (Walton, 2010; Pilling, 2012). We might be able to link these processes of digestion with the mapping of the origin of Beckett's focus on femininity on stage, starting with the text presented on 10 October 1960 in a letter to Bray as 'Female Solo Play', 'the imbedded female solo machine' that inaugurates a trajectory going from *Happy Days* to *Play*, *Not I*, and *Footfalls* (Beckett, 2014, 364–5; Beckett, 1960; UoR MS1227).

The unbearable Mitchell correspondence confronts us with loss, at least for now: Beckett's loss of his brother, Mitchell's loss of Beckett's love, the melancholic attempt at keeping the life of the relationship alive in the safety of the spatial and temporal distance marking its loss, and our own mourning of Beckett as the idealised subject of criticism. The Mitchell correspondence shows our investment in the archive as a space of reparation, which it cannot always provide.

3 Biting, Swallowing, and All This Stuff

murmuring, Imagine him kissing, caressing, licking, sucking, fucking and buggering all this stuff, no sound.

(Beckett, 2010b, 75)

All heaven in the sphincter
the sphincter

(Beckett, 2012, 12)

3.1 Sullied Images

In 1956 Les Éditions de Minuit published *L'image* by Jean de Berg (later identified as Catherine Robbe-Grillet), provocatively dedicated to and prefaced by Pauline Réage. Réage (Anne Desclos's nom de plume) was the author of *The Story of O*, published in 1954 by Jean-Jacques Pauvert, who between 1956 and 1958 was put on trial 'for being the first to publish Sade officially without using a fake name (his edition of the *120 journées* was published in 1948)' (Baroghel, 2018, 215).[5] Criticism has recently re-evaluated Beckett's complex relation with Sade: we know that Beckett's library contained an unmarked copy of *L'Œuvre du Marquis de Sade* (1909) introduced by Apollinaire, in addition to books by Alain Robbe-Grillet, Maurice Blanchot and Ludovic Janvier, the theorist of the *nouveau roman* (Friedman, 1960; Van Hulle and Nixon, 2013, 56). In 1938 Beckett almost translated *Les 120 journeés* for Obelisk Press, but sensibly refused to yield to the temptation. Near the end of 1950 Beckett started to 'read, compile, and translate selected French language texts in dialogue with Duthuit' for a special issue of *transition* on Sade, which was never published (Krimper, 2022, 1). In 1972, writing to George Reavey, he tentatively credited Apollinaire with starting it all: 'he must have been the initiator of the Sade boom' (Beckett, 2016, 305–6). John Pilling, Shane Weller, Jean-Michel Rabaté, Michael Krimper, and Elsa Baroghel's studies have changed our way of thinking about Sade in Beckett. Laura Salisbury on the role of sadism in relation to the joke and Eleanor Green on the relation between Sade and the 1960s prose have proven transformative. Here, I want to think of de Berg's *L'image* as part of the Parisian Sade boom: often described as minimalist pornography or pornographic *nouveau roman*, de Berg's homonymous 1954 novel is remarkable for its intense preoccupation with the arrangement of Anne's passive body and Claire's directorial control for the satisfaction of Jean's and Claire's sadistic drives – the discussion of the much later *Catastrophe* in Section 2.2 has touched

---

[5] It was later discovered that Desclos was in a relationship with Jean Poulhan, Sade enthusiast and editor of the *Nouvelle Revue Française* from 1925 to 1940 and from 1946 to 1968 (Sontag, 1967).

on similar concerns in Beckett's political drama, and the next section will come back to this issue.

'More theatrical than novelistic', de Berg's is soft Sade: entirely devoid of what Beckett described to Duthuit in 1952 as 'all those turds and sucked rectums', it foregrounds the aesthetic and imaginative elements of eroticism by stretching them beyond any principle of verisimilitude – it is an image after all (Beckett, 2011, 311). Jean, for instance, thinks the blood flowing from the deeper scars in Claire's photographs of Anne must be artificial, while only the 'prettiest' little scars will mark her body; ultimately, it does not matter, since Anne's body, like Justine's, magically heals itself only to be tortured again (de Berg, 1956; Bersani, 1976, 308). In the most excruciatingly self-reflective moments of the novel, Jean, a critic and connoisseur (who moves from the position of spectator to that of perpetrator), is preoccupied that some of Claire's arrangements are either too romantic (a rose secured to Anne's inner thigh via its thorn) or too gothic (whipping and chaining Anne against marble columns). The novel 'keeps the cliché opposition between spectacle and spectator intact' and sanctions the 'myth of a difference of nature between passion and intelligence, or between desire and interpretive fantasy, or, finally, between art and criticism' (Bersani, 1976, 309).

Eleanor Green has demonstrated the importance of reading the 1960s prose as part of the contemporary concerns in French literature and art with minimalism and the question of sexual limits (Green, 2022). Before her, Conor Carville explored this issue in relation to the visual arts (Carville, 2018). Three years after Minuit published de Berg, Beckett's *L'image* (1959) can be seen as responding to some of the current *nouveau roman* preoccupations with the flattening of characters and plot, establishing the self-sufficiency of the work, and exploring the need to separate eroticism from both the romantic and the gothic traditions. The contrast between the two images of de Berg and Beckett, however, shows how an apparent confluence of preoccupations with minimalism and sadism leads to almost opposite results. Beckett's *L'image* builds on previous forms of de-idealisation of the love object, questions the reassertion of mastery put under threat by the possibility of the heterosexual encounter, undoes the opposition between looking at doing (criticism and art), and paves the way towards *How It Is*'s incorporation and expulsion of sadism.

Composed in March 1959, sent to Mary Hutchinson and published in November in the first issue of the English magazine *X: A Quarterly Review*, edited by David Wright and Patrick Swift, the short prose was part of the author's work towards *Comment c'est*, which Beckett had begun in December 1958. It was later incorporated, with a number of variants, as versets 150–71 of the final version of the longer text (Beckett, 1959; Pilling, 2006, 145 and 148).[6] Here, I am going to analyse predominantly its English translation by Edith Fournier and compare it to Beckett's French original and its variants in *Comment c'est.*

In *The Image* we encounter heterosexual young love, seen through a mirror effect:

> I look to me about sixteen and to top it all glorious weather egg blue sky and scamper of little clouds I have my back turned to me and the girl too whom I hold by the hand the arse I have judging by the flowers that deck the emerald grass we are in April or in May I don't know and how glad I am to ignore the reasons why I abide by these stories of flowers and seasons. (Beckett, 1995, 166)[7]

Something is not quite right in this romantic image: 'these stories of flowers and seasons' consist mainly of clichés ('to top it all up', 'glorious weather', 'emerald grass') and hand holding. They are briefly interrupted by 'the arse I have' ('le cul que j'ai') before the narrator continues with the appraisal of the seasonal weather. The surprising observation might suggest either the interchangeable quality of 'hand' and 'arse' ('whom I hold by the hand / the arse'), with its clash of registers, or establish an incongruous relation between the flowers and the size of the younger self's posterior ('the arse I have / judging by the flowers'). If we opt for reading the sentence as an aside to oneself ('whom I hold by the hand / the arse I have / judging by the flowers'), then the sentence acts as an almost mechanical blip, a bit of static that reminds us that the romantic image is an artificial assemblage.[8] The later *Ping* (1966) made this its own narrative method through a hiccup rhythm: 'long lashes imploring ping silence ping over' (Beckett, 1995, 196). By including, like a mechanical blip, a remark that is almost childish in its mildly transgressive pleasure (as if one cheekily shouted 'cul!' in the middle of a sentence), the text encourages a humorous reflection on the voyeuristic, objectifying, and narcissistic pleasure of looking back at one's younger self – indeed, at one's younger backside (the preoccupation with ageing buttocks' lack of elasticity resurfaces in *How It Is*). With Clov, we might say 'we too were bonny – once. It's a rare thing not to have been bonny – once', but any nostalgic sentimentality that the play undercuts through

---

[6] The Minuit 1988 version offers variants. It was anonymously translated into English and published in 1990 by Calder in *As the Story Was Told*, 'which occasioned a flurry of disapproving letters' (Cohn, 2005, 253). The version in the *Complete Shorter Prose*, edited by S. E. Gontarski (Beckett, 1995), which I use here, offers the English text in the translation by Edith Fournier. Ruby Cohn used her own translation.

[7] The 2009 Faber edition reads: 'whom I hold who holds me by the hand the arse I have / we are if I may believe the colours that deck the emerald grass if I may believe them we are old dream. Of flowers and seasons we are' (Beckett, 2009b, 23).

[8] For a discussion of Tourette's syndrome in Beckett, see Simpson (2022b); Barry, Maude and Salisbury (2016, 127–35); Lesnik-Oberstein (2017, 10).

comedy is instead spoiled in *The Image*. Writing to Donald McWhinnie on 7 March 1958 (Pilling dates the composition of *L'Image* to the fortnight before a letter to Mary Hutchinson on 28 March), Beckett described the 'short stage monologue' which became *Krapp's Last Tape* as 'a rather sentimental affair in my best original English manner', a statement that facilitates a reading of *L'Image* as its French corrective (Pilling, 2006, 145; Beckett, 2014, 115).

In his analysis of the role of what he calls 'the philosophical image' in Beckett, Anthony Uhlmann refers to Gilles Deleuze's point in *L'Epuisé*, who claimed that 'it is extremely difficult to make a pure and unsullied image, one that is nothing but image' (Uhlmann, 2006, 34–5; Beckett, 1992, 158). Deleuze owes a debt to a romantic tradition for which the purity of the image is a goal, despite its acknowledged impossibility, but in Beckett the scepticism is much stronger: 'Such a harmony only he can relish whose long experience [is] such as to permit a perfect mental image of the entire system. But it is doubtful that such a one exists', the anthropologist-as-narrator opines a few years later in *The Lost Ones* (Beckett, 1995, 204; Carville, 2018, 237). It is not a coincidence that the interruption of the budding heterosexual romance involves the term 'arse'. In *The Image*, the phrase 'the arse I had' retains a little of the innocence on which the text focuses, but the same words ('arse' / 'cul') are linked to the central role of anality in *How It Is*.

To think about sexuality in this text, I build on Salisbury's work on digestion and expulsion in relation to comedy and psychoanalysis, as demonstrated through her reading of Beckett's notes on Ernest Jones and Otto Rank (whom Beckett nicknamed 'Erogenous Jones' and 'Freudchen') and his psychoanalytic treatment with Bion (Salisbury, 2011, 72; Feldman, 2006, 97, 100). Central to my discussion is also Peter Boxall's understanding of a continuity between the comic ode to the arsehole in *Molloy* ('"we underestimate this little hole, it seems to me, we call it the arse-hole and affect to despise it", the novel musically intones') and the way in which *How It is* 'is entirely dominated by the slithery s/m erotics of Pim and his band of victims and tormentors who crawl through the mud prodding each other's anuses with can openers' (Boxall, 2004, 114–18). *How It Is* often collapses the difference between arse and anus: when the wife 'Pam Prim' is evoked, the couple 'tried to revive' their dwindling interest in sex 'through the arse too late' ('par le cul trop tard') while the text's 'midget grammar' ('grammaire d'oiseau') also goes 'plof down the hole' (Beckett, 2009b, 66) ('floc dans le trou'; 120). When we read 'stab him simply in the arse that is to say speak' (61) we are not spectating but made complicit in the torture that this text enacts when asking to be made sense of it, to find 'answers' and 'proof'. When the language itself disappears down the hole/orifice, it reverts to a logic in which the anus is 'a bar to connectedness, rather than anything that opens up new channels of communication. It is preferred to the mouth because, unlike the mouth, it doesn't speak', as Boxall put it after Bersani (Boxall, 2004, 114–18). In the shorter text, the interrupting, comic 'arse' is just a blip in communication, rather than central to the breaking down of the opposition between mouth and anus in *How It Is*, whose 'digestive circularity' is a formal structuring principle: speech turns into matter, which turns into speech, and so forth (Caselli, 2005a, 169).

This difference is important because it is tempting to read *The Image* as simply a portion of *How It Is*, doing something very similar: after all, it establishes the images as 'vistas' ('perspectives' in the original French) in the middle of the mud which impairs speech: 'The tongue gets clogged with mud only one remedy then pull in and suck it swallow the mud or spit question to know whether it is nourishing and vistas' (165). However, Ruby Cohn was right when she wrote that 'For all the unpunctuated, unconcatenated phrases, that image is incisively etched': there is a clear split between the production of the image and the image itself (Cohn, 2005, 254). Such separation will work very differently in *How It Is*, because the text oscillates between the impossibility of full, transparent meaning – the illusory immediacy of the image – and the muddy materiality of its language which attempts, and fails, to be just mud and muck, to make no sense, developing on the page an aesthetic problem that existed at least since *Endgame*: 'We're not beginning to … to … mean something?' (Beckett, 2006, 108). If, as Uhlmann writes, the process of creating an image 'is strongly tied to the idea of relation and nonrelation', in *How It Is* the mechanism of transmission of speech and the 'imbrication' of bodies make singularity and relationality equally impossible and impossible to avoid (Uhlmann, 2006, 35; Wolff, 2008, 119–36).

In *The Image*, relationality works in two ways: on the one hand, the 'perspective'/'vista' is a clearly etched image of a young man and woman going on a picnic; on the other, the digestive mechanism of *How It Is* begins to make itself felt but is still contained through the heterosexual young couple rather than performed through the digestive and evacuating processes of the text itself (Caselli, 2005a; Walton, 2010; Salisbury, 2012):

> and here we are again eating sandwiches alternate bites I mine she hers and exchanging endearments my sweet girl I bite she swallows my sweet boy she bites I swallow we don't yet coo with our bills full my darling girl I bite she swallows my darling boy she bites I swallow brief fog' (Beckett, 1995, 167).

The staged innocence of the passage – two adolescents are holding hands and eating sandwiches against the backdrop of a pastoral Springtime landscape – transforms itself under our eyes, through repetition, into something quite different, as the French original perhaps shows even more incisively: 'mon amour je morde elle avale mon trésor elle mord j'avale' (Beckett, 1959, 47). The coupling of 'she bites I swallow' and 'I bite she swallows', with its symmetrical arrangement and repetitious endearments, cannot avoid being suggestive, pointing to something outside of itself, shattering the possibility of a non-relational image. The text forces us, in ways that might be experienced as funny, unpleasant, or both, to ask ourselves what exactly we are looking at, right now.

In his early notes from Karin Stephen's *Psychoanalysis and Medicine: A Study of the Wish to Fall Ill*, Beckett notes the cycle of 'disappointment of desire, aggression, fear of results, object of desire turned into something terrifying, repudiation, disappointment, etc.', something that *The Image* seems to enact (qtd in Feldman, 2006, 110). The girl is suddenly ugly (she is 'hideous' in Beckett's translation for *How It Is*; Beckett, 2009b, 24); it doesn't seem to matter, since the 'I' tells us that it is 'not with her that I am concerned', but 'me' described as: 'pale starting hair red pudding face with pimples protruding belly gaping fly spindle legs wide astraddle for greater stability knocking at the knees feet splayed thirty-five degrees minimum fatuous half smile to posterior horizon figuring the morn of life green tweeds yellow boots cowslip or suchlike in the buttonhole' (Beckett, 1995, 166–7).

This 'perspective' is still firmly anchored in a first-person narrative, so the link between heterosexual encounters and disgust becomes a variation of what we encountered in *First Love* and *Molloy* with the puppet-like motion reminiscent of *Watt*'s walk. Disgust soon turns into hatred towards the object of desire while the 'I' desires his own self-destruction: 'I feel like shouting plant her there and run cut your throat' (Beckett, 1995, 167) / 'j'ai envie de crier plaque-la là et cours t'ouvrir les veines' (Beckett, 1959, 35–6), preannouncing the end of the image itself: 'now it's done I've done the image' (Beckett, 1995, 168), which became in *How It Is* the less suggestive 'I've had the image' (Beckett, 2009b, 25), 'j'ai eu l'image' (Beckett, 1961, 48).

The publication history of *The Image* is itself part of a digestive process, as it is eventually incorporated by the larger organism. In *How It Is* the grammatical 'I' no longer coalesces in a subject but is 'a kind of stopping point for voices, an intersection of extortionary speech acts, a collective depot for all the words whose source of transmission remains uncertain' or, in the words of the text itself 'an orgy of false beings' (Bersani and Dutoit, 1993, 60; Beckett, 2009b, 59). Shane Weller and Eleanor Green are right in claiming that the novel is not 'sadism pure and simple': it digests and expels Sade (as it does Dante) (Weller, 2008; Green, 2022, 39). The 'rigour of composition' is there in the geometrical structure and turned into mud to be spat out or swallowed; the logic of torture is pushed to its limits and experienced as unbearable (the 'unbearable thump on skull' and the 'unbearable opener'); a sexualised body part and language become interchangeable in a moment of stalled progression ('arse or capitals if he has lost the thread'; Beckett, 2009b, 65). Both hard and flaccid (there is nothing soft about this muddy text), *How It Is* brings together a 'furious orality', 'as if a non-digestible difference could be chewed and swallowed into sameness', with an equally furious anality: the 'despised arse-hole' is the link 'between me and the other excrements' (Bersani, 2018, viii; Boxall, 2004, 119). As Boxall has argued, the can opener tries to breach the anus's 'excretionary muteness' and yet attempts (and fails) to use it as 'a portal and as a link between one's being and the rest of the world' (Boxall, 2004, 118).

The two texts map a shift from a heterosexual 'image' of romance 'spoiled' by biting and swallowing to a text intensely sexualised in its anal organisation but no longer underpinned by sexual relations structured around gender polarities. We are not looking at a post-gendered world but at the closest that Beckett gave us to a sexual organism. *How It Is* bites and swallows, explores with the tongue, spits, expels, and introjects. Mouth and anus operate as the entry and exit points of language and matter, speech and silence (Caselli, 2005a, 148). The trajectory from *The Image* to *How It Is* goes from the cracked mirror held to the heterosexual romantic image to the convulsive receptiveness and hostility of a sexual organism.

Writing to Patrick Magee in February 1960, Beckett anticipates a disgusted reaction to *How It Is*:

> What will meet your disgusted eye is a series of short paragraphs (average 4 or 5 lines) separated by pauses during which panting cordially invited and without as much punctuation as a comma to break the monotony or promote the understanding. [...] I have made the writing as clear as such dreadful circumstances permit, but I intend also to have the goodness to point the copy I shall be sending you in a fortnight or three weeks for now. It is I think a microphone text, to be murmured, and if you agree with me I hope it will be possible for you to use one, notwithstanding the liveliness of the occasion. I have never committed anything – I trust – so exhausted and unpalatable and shall not be in the least offended if you refuse to have anything to do with it. (Beckett, 2014, 306)

Despite its caution, the letter is suggestive, complicit, and intimate; the 'pauses during which panting cordially invited' and the murmuring hint at a sexual excitement connected counterintuitively to monotony, absence, and complexity. Written in a language as clear as mud (these are, after all, the dreadful circumstances of the text), the 'horribly difficult' *How It Is* needs happening but carries with it a whiff of guilt (Beckett 'committed' it).[9] Departing from the stripped-down Protestant aesthetic about which Beckett could joke to Duthuit in 1951, this is a very Parisian text, which speaks to key post-war debates on the relation between the mechanised repetition of technology and its effect on sexual life, the image as an entry point to rethink literary aesthetics, and sadism as a way to abandon character and retheorise perspective (Beckett, 2011, 318). Unlike de Berg's *L'Image*, *How It Is* (and, to a lesser extent, Beckett's own *L'Image* before it) refuses to keep in place the opposition between spectator and spectacle, which in de Berg supports the heterosexual divide of power. Paradoxically, the rejection of a split between desire and intelligence is one of the reasons why *How It Is* has proven historically too complex to arouse, unlike Beckett's predictions to Magee. A sexual, hungry organism emerging from an infinite passing of language/faeces received and expelled, *How It Is* is a unique attempt at incorporating indigestible material: it is certainly 'unpalatable'. Its convulsions are exciting as much as they are exhausting.

3.2 Bleached Dirt

> Walls and ceiling flaking plaster or suchlike, floor like bleached dirt, aha, something there, leave it for the moment.
>
> (Beckett, 1995, 173)

After the furious excitation of *How It Is*, the prose moved from excremental darkness towards a dessicated whiteness, from lubricious convulsions to 'tremors' (Salisbury, 2012). The theatre staged sexual disappointment through the coupling of spatial immobility and either verbal ferocity (*Play*, whose idea 'excite[d]' him 'immoderately', as Beckett told Alan Schneider in 1962; Beckett, 1998, 122) or desperate light-heartedness (*Happy Days*), made us experience the gendered materiality of speech (*Not I*), and reframed sadism in political terms (*Catastrophe*). The post–*How It Is* prose instead demanded 'that we make do with little' (Salisbury, 2012, 148). This is a return to the 'quiescence of the inorganic world' after the 'momentary extinction of a highly intensified excitation', which Freud connects to the sexual act (Freud, 1920, 62). Mladen Dolar and Laura Salisbury have demonstrated the importance of the death drive to this intermittent process of diminution, not as 'a morbid fascination with death' but understood as a 'thrust of persistence which cannot be annihilated' (Dolar, 2010, 64, 61; Salisbury, 2012, 163, 71–2; Salisbury, 2023).[10] This

---

[9] See also Beckett's 'Psychology Notes' on Ernest Jones, TCD10971/8/22 and TCD 10971/8/23 (see Feldman, 2006, 111).

[10] In his reading of the 'Psychology Notes' (TCD MS10971), Feldman tells us Beckett encountered 'Instinct and Their Vicissitudes' (1915) in 1934 when reading Ernest Jones' *Papers on Psychoanalysis* (Feldman, 2006, 78–115).

section attends to this thrust of persistence by showing how the 'very little' of the late prose becomes rather a lot – even too much – once we start thinking about sexuality (Berlant, 2000; Cohn, 2005, 289). It will do so by looking at the strange desire for intimacy in *All Strange Away* before analysing the role of the 'almost sentimental' in *Company*.

The 'first in a series in which objects and figures are arranged and rearranged in confined spaces with mathematical precision', *All Strange Away* has been linked to minimalism and abstraction (Gontarski, 1995, xxx; Nixon, 2010, xiii). Eleanor Green has demonstrated how the 'disappearing act' enacted by the text, and more generally by the 1960s prose, has blinded us to the sheer volume of 'explicit sex acts' present in this period (Green, 2022, 12–15). Before her, Graham Fraser discussed the role of what he called, after Susan Sontag, the text's 'pornographic imagination' (Sontag, 1967; Fraser, 1995, 515–30; Carville, 2018, 235–8). *All Strange Away* enumerates body parts and sex acts in a language that made even the most scrupulous of commentators vacillate: Cohn described Emma as 'lovely beyond words' while the grammatical subject is not Emma but her body parts as perceived by a perspective temporary anchored to a masculine pronoun: 'First face alone, lovely beyond words, leave it at that, then deasil breasts alone, then thighs and cunt alone, then arse and hole alone, all lovely beyond words' (Beckett, 2010b, 75). The graphic blazon is nevertheless part of a text, as Cohn astutely noted, 'nostalgic for an intimacy that may be achieved only in fancy' (Cohn, 2005, 289).

All Strange Away performs the desire for an intimacy which is both sexual and textual by sending us back to another text in which alleged distinctions between sexed bodies, gender identity and sexual desire break down: James Joyce's 'Circe' section in *Ulysses*. Emmo and Emma, with their fantasies of submission, intense 'fancying', and 'cold copulation', are a rewriting of Bella and Bello in Joyce's 'pornosophical philotheology', 'Nighttown' (which, as Section 2.1 explained, played a major role in *Dream*). This interpretation reshapes the widely held opinion that *Molloy* marks 'the end of "Joyceology"' and reinscribes it in a queer, rather than oedipal, logic (Wimbush, 2018, 95). Building on Deleuze and Guattari's reading of 'the literature a minority makes in a major language' as deterritorialised language, Lauren Berlant has argued that 'as with minor literatures, minor intimacies have been forced to develop aesthetics of the extreme to push these spaces into being by way of small and grand gestures' (Deleuze and Guattari, 1983, 16; Berlant, 2000, 5). My reading of *All Strange Away* as a 'minor intimacy' allows us to see how the prose work makes the grand gesture of returning to Joyce while at the same time rendering it small, constraining it into increasingly confined spaces: the nostalgia for 'Circe' no longer leads to *Dream*'s 'verbal coprotechnics' but creates a strange kind of intimacy, attainable only in fancy.

The 'Nighttown' episode, we may remember, is also suffused with nostalgia: it opens by looking back to a late nineteenth-century descent into the underworld, in which figures emerge from shadows, the circus takes centre stage, and Bloom is a flâneur. The 'lovelorn longlost lugubry Booloohoom' and its opposite, the 'fatchuck cheekchops of Jollypoldy the rixdix doldy' (Joyce, 1922, 413) reflected in the hairdresser's window are soon caught in a series of dark fantasies of persecution, in which Bloom is described in front of an imaginary tribunal to be 'bisexually abnormal' by Dr Mulligan and 'a finished example of the new womanly man' by Dr Dixon (465). The pathologisation of desire prepares the ground for the encounter with Bella Cohen: the novel describes her as 'a massive whoremistress' (494), familiar and threatening in equal measure. This is followed by Bloom's expression of his desire to be dominated (496), his fears of impotence (501), and ultimately to the radical instability of gendered identity when engaged in sexual acts in which his fantasies of submissions are predominant (502) and during which he acquires a female pronoun.

'Nighttown' gradually moves from excitement, hilarity, and sheer fun to despair via the hanged croppy boy (refigured in *Waiting for Godot*'s joke about hanging and erections), the encounter with the soldiers, and the conclusion in which Bloom looks after Stephen and takes him home, pretending that everything is 'above bawd' with Corny Kelleher. The episode's trajectory is both progressive and cyclical: climax is followed by post-coital sadness, while the Vico-like circularity of which Beckett wrote in 1929 can also be observed in the ghost of the dead son Rudy, resurrecting tropes (chthonic descent, ghostly infants) belonging more to the 1880s than either 1904 or 1922. We move on and yet are stuck, like Bloom and his unposted letter to Bella Cohen – a magnificent example of a drunken Uncle Charles principle (Kenner, 1978, 15–38): 'Exuberant female. Enormously I desiderate your domination. I am exhausted, abandoned, no more young. I stand, so to speak, with an unposted letter bearing the extra regulation fee before the too late box of the general postoffice of human life' (Joyce, 1922, 496). The language is fun, drunk (a quality that in *Work in Progress* earned Beckett's praise in 1929), and destabilising in its ability to stage fantasies of persecution, mastery and domination. Bella/Bello and Bloom/Ruby are no longer attached to their stated gender identities when acting their fantasies: the pathologised 'bisexually abnormal', the culturally stigmatised 'new womanly man' revels in the sexual pleasure and pain opened up by his occupying a feminine position.

Trans theory has given us the tools to read 'Nighttown' as a seriously funny exploration of the very material role played by fantasy in the construction of both gender identity and sexual orientation. Bloom sheds 'male garments' (Joyce, 1922, 436) and confesses to having tried on Marion/Molly's clothes only once – washing them 'to save the laundry bill' as a form of 'the purest thrift' we are assured (437), showing us how the 'assimilation of misogynist stereotypes' so often raised as a spectre by transexclusionary thinkers becomes here 'the rule governing all gender' (Long Chu, 2019, 22). Bloom is Ruby and needs Bella to be Bello: in the provocative words of Andrea Long Chu, 'we are all females and we all hate it' (23). Long Chu has reinterpreted Catharine MacKinnon's thesis that men and women are constructed 'through an eroticization of domination and submission' in the context of trans theory: 'if there is any lesson of gender transition – from the simplest request regarding pronouns to the most invasive surgeries – it's that gender is something other people *give* you. Gender exists, if it exists at all, only in the structural generosity of strangers' (24). 'Nighttown' possesses such generosity: Bloom/Ruby and Bella/Bello enable each other to become 'a canvas for someone else's fantasy' (20). Such generosity, however, is underpinned by the transactional economy of sex work and confined to the darkness of the night: 'Nighttown' makes us participate in Bloom's excitement in the temporary undoing of gender identity through sexual desire but at the price of confining it to a particular time and space and containing it through the fantasies that sex work liberates.

All Strange Away moves from darkness to the 'frenzy of the visible' in the desiccated landscape of post-Sadean writing, well past the moment in which reading Sade is 'less staggering than the first time, glimpsed in the half-light of uncut pages' (Beckett, 2011, 311). Fancy is declared dead while incited. We have a deviser, a super-egoic director, at times momentarily funny and self-congratulatory ('all six planes hot when shining, aha'; Beckett, 2010b, 74) but often short to the point of becoming censorious ('No sound', 'leave it for the moment', 74). Carville has noted how the imagination is aligned with activity (Emmo) and fancy with passivity (Emma), suggesting a 'deep implication of traditional categories of the aesthetic in gendered power relations and the appetites of the libido' (Carville, 2018, 235). James Hansford has pointed out that this alignment is complicated by fantasy, since 'Emma *fancies* herself the passive partner in sexual activities whereas Emmo *imagined* himself its active instigator' (Hansford, 1983, 53; Cohn, 2005, 287). Both readings conflate the observer with Emmo, but the observer is first a 'he'; then the 'he' seems to be working in place of an undecidability 'or hers since sex not seen so far'; later, the perspective becomes that of 'say Emma standing, turning' and 'Emmo on the walls', fancying her passive role in relation to Emmo: 'she turns murmuring, Fancy her being all kissed, licked, sucked fucked and so on by all that, no sound' (Beckett, 2010b, 76). Eventually, we are told that there is 'no Emmo, no need, never was' (76).

Fantasies of activity and passivity are linked to gender identity, but we are not sure whether the observer, a 'he' at this point, murmurs to himself 'Imagine him kissing etc', in the third person (No, he!) or if the narrative voice tells us that he murmurs and then encourages us to imagine him engaged in sexual acts: it all hangs on a comma. In both cases both imagination and fancy need a split, which the projection of the body parts on the wall provides. The difference between Emma and Emmo sustains, momentarily, the fantasy of heterosexual inter-course, shown not to be fully anchored to gender, albeit more firmly linked to masculine and feminine positions than in Joyce.

In a 1958 letter to Aidan Higgins focused on a male narrator describing the interiority of a female character, Beckett tried to praise a narration from 'without': 'The memorable description of Emily May's service is more convincing, and more revealing of her "cose segrete" than your effort at incursion thereinto' (Beckett, 2014, 142–3). 'Nighttown' as a revelation of the 'cose segrete' conceptualised sexual fantasies as a depth to be explored, without any trace of Protestant prudishness and with a considerable amount of jouissance. Emma and Emmo are assembled architectonically: their 'hot projections' take place on the intermittently cold walls of a cube or a rotunda. The text's aesthetics is of surfaces, not depths, which has been connected to the pornographical by Graham Fraser (1995), Conor Carville (2018) and Eleanor Green (2022): in *All Strange Away* 'pornography is what it feels like when you think you have an object, but really the object has *you*' (Long Chu, 2019, 21).

Of Bella's monumental domination nothing more than a 'strand of Emma's motte' seems to remain: an odd object (albeit not an entirely unfamiliar one), as noted by Carville, belonging to the order of the fly (also present), and perform-ing a similar function to that of the *memento mori* insect on a piece of fruit or a flower in an early modern still life: a minor gesture and a grand statement at once.[11] We are basically clutching at straws in this 'torrent of hope and unhope mingled and submission amounting to nothing' (Beckett, 2010b, 78). In both texts, gender fails to work as a successful policing of the border of difference, as an 'accumulation strategy', despite the more radical dissolution of boundaries in 'Nighttown' (Gabriel, 2020). In both texts, this is achieved through sexual fantasies involving active and passive roles, submission and domination, but while in *Ulysses* we had to plunge in, drunkenly, and emerge with a hangover and a sense of nostalgia, in *All Strange Away* we must watch ourselves watching – we have to become the object we thought we had.

---

[11] A Madame de la Motte makes an appearance in 'Sanies II' (Beckett, 2012, 14); Pam Prim 'se raiset la motte' in *Comment c'est* (Beckett, 1961, 119).

The text's 'cold copulation' cannot abandon itself to either fancy or imagination. Intimacies are often 'formed around threats to the image of the world [they] seek to sustain', but *All Strange Away* as a minor intimacy recognises itself to be a threat to Joyce's 'Nighttown' (Berlant, 2000, 7). Beckett stages a strange nostalgia for a world in which desire could still be figured as depth, a descent into the darkness of the psyche in which sexual pleasure undoes the self as a gendered identity.

'Nighttown' is the containing space within which the intimacy with one's aggression and passivity could be feared, joyfully celebrated, and acted upon. *All Strange Away* seems unable to forget that there was a price to pay to achieve this: in early Beckett, as argued in Section 2.1, there was an unresolved acknowledgement of the problems with both the glorification and the erasure of the sex worker's labour for literature. *All Strange Away*, a minor intimacy, never allows us to forget that sex – and not just sex work – performs important work for both fancy and imagination, even if that is little more than a 'tremor of sorrow for faint memory of a lying side by side and fancy murmured dead' (Beckett, 2010b, 84).

3.3 The Filthy Eye of Flesh

> Touch? The thrust of the ground against his bones. All the way from the calcaneum to bump of philoprogenitiveness. Might not a notion to stir ruffle his apathy? To turn on his side.
>
> (Beckett, 2009a, 33)

> Slow systole diastole. And the body that scandal. While its sole hands in view. On its sole pubis.
>
> (Beckett, 2009a, 60)

There is a strange proximity between the sexual and the sentimental in *Company*, Beckett's book of origins. To speak about sentimentality in Beckett is counterintuitive, but critics have noted the uneasy presence of 'moving scenes', 'almost sentimental evocations', and 'miniaturised tenderness' in childhood memories, remembrances about parents, and early love – all subjects covered by *Company* and presenting considerable risks for any writer (Caselli, 2005b, 273). There has been a justified reluctance to label the text as straightforwardly sentimental, however: Enoch Brater persuasively claimed that there is 'no trace of sloppy sentimentality' in this text (Brater, 1994, 169–70), but his defence champions the seriously literary against the mawkish, a reassuring opposition that *Company* complicates and one that feminist and queer theorists have convincingly critiqued (Radway, 1984; Clark, 1991; Fox, 1994, 146–201; Berlant, 2008).

Company places the sexual and the sentimental in a relation of uncomfortable proximity. It accepts the risk of inevitable sentimentality which remembering one's life entails but brings us back, again and again, to the problem that 'sentimentality [...] contains a denial of hate', as Donald Winnicott wrote in 1949 (Winnicot, 1949, 73). *Company* shows what 'miniaturised tenderness' can achieve but makes it unnervingly close to the sexual, so that it never allows us to forget what the sentimental is likely to occlude.

The 'you' remembers being in the 'bloom of adulthood. Imagine a whiff of that. On your back in the dark you remember. Ah, you you remember. Cloudless May day' (Beckett, 2009a, 25). The repetition of the 'you' creates the nervous possibility of the sentimental, for which 'bloom of adulthood' had prepared the ground, soon undercut by the wordplay 'Imagine a whiff of that'. The lover, a 'she', 'joins you in the little summerhouse', whose proportions are carefully set out. The text continues:

> There on summer Sundays after his midday meal your father loved to retreat with *Punch* and a cushion. The waist of his trousers unbuttoned he sat on the one ledge turning the pages. You on the other with your feet dangling. When he chuckled you tried to chuckle too. When his chuckle died yours too. That you should try to imitate his chuckle pleased and tickled him greatly and sometimes he would chuckle for no other reason than to hear you try to chuckle too. [...] The years have flown and there at the same place as then you sit in the bloom of adulthood bathed in rainbow light gazing before you. She is late. You close your eyes and try to calculate the volume. Simple sums you find a help in times of trouble. (Beckett, 2009a, 25–6)

The summer house enables the 'you' to set up the comparison between his younger self, a boy trying to please his father, and the father's pleasure in realising this, with the waiting for his lover. The two episodes are clearly separated by the almost sentimental expression 'the years have flown', which is soon rebalanced by another mathematical dissection, this time connected to the sexual in ways that bring us back to the arranged bodies of *All Strange Away*: 'knowing from experience that the height or length you have in common is the sum of equal segments. For when bolt upright or lying full stretch you cleave face to face then your knees meet and your pubes and the hairs of your heads mingle' (26–7).[12]

Such temporal and spatial separation is, however, short-lived once the lover arrives:

> The ruby lips do not return your smile. Your gaze descends to the breasts. You do not remember them so big. To the abdomen. Same impression. Dissolve to

---

[12] See also *Ill Seen Ill Said* (Beckett, 2009a, 60). On the sentence's Dantean overtones, see Caselli (2005a, 204).

> your father's straining against the unbuttoned waistband. Can it be that she is with child without you having asked as much as her hand? You go back into your mind. She too did you but know it has closed her eyes. So you sit face to face in the little summerhouse. With eyes closed and your hands on your pubes. In that rainbow light. That dead still. (27)

The 'you' acts as a director, instructing himself to use the camera/mind's eye to 'dissolve to your father's straining against the unbuttoned waistband'. Earlier, the 'you' had been described as sitting on the ledge with his father, who had the 'waist of his trousers unbuttoned'; here, the father is straining against the unbuttoned waistband (the French text reads 'Il [ventre] se fond dans celui de ton père débordant de la ceinture débutonnée'; Beckett, 1985, 57). The use of the determinate article creates a familiarity between the two slightly different formulation; through this familiarity, *Company* revisits the relation between frail masculinity and overwhelming femininity which we have observed in many of the pre-1960s works. Instead of leading to the disgust and aggression encountered in the three novels and the novellas, however, here the father's straining stomach echoes the previous sexual encounters that the potential pregnancy might betray, reverberating with the fear of pregnancy which characterises, as Paul Stewart has demonstrated, much of the early oeuvre. The unbuttoned waistband also anticipates the sex act that will follow, merging the present into both past and future.

This 'sensation of asynchrony' that I want to theorise, with Elizabeth Freeman, 'as a queer phenomenon [. . .] experienced as a mode of erotic difference', is one of the ways in which this 'philoprogenitive' text shows the residual presence of the sexual in the most culturally accepted form of boy's love, that for his father: if it is a form of queering, it is one that owes more to a psychoanalytic logic than a progressive political agenda. Kadji Amin's challenge against 'the tendency, within Queer Studies, to equate naming an object *queer* with claiming, for it, an unequivocally positive political value' can be put to good use to understand this 'disturbing attachment' (Freeman, 2007; Amin, 2017, 115; Keeling, 2019, 87; Stacey, 2019). Although I reject, as explained earlier, any easy parallel between Genet and Beckett, Amin's critical daringness can help us explore the eye/camera dissolving between heterosexual sex acts and the memory of one's father. After all, *Company* is not the first of Beckett's prose works exploring such attachments in ways that remain recalcitrant to any form of 'redemptive perversion'. Eleanor Green has addressed the disturbing cross-generational exploration of mastery and subjection via sexuality in *Enough*, which Beckett claimed to have written 'aberrantly' (Green, 2022, 221–65; Nixon, 2010, xiv).

Company pushes the impetus to dissolve between the two scenes to its logical consequence by dissolving the syntactical integrity of what follows. 'She too did you but know it has closed her eyes' seems to suggest that, not unlike the 'you' but without him knowing, she went into her mind, an interpretation supported by the French 'Elle aussi à ton insu a fermé les yeux' (Beckett, 1985, 58).[13] The grammar in the English final text is uncharacteristically tortuous, however, suggesting a sexual meaning – 'she too did you' – which implies reciprocity and, at a stretch, even promiscuity. 'Did you but know' indicates lack of knowledge but goes in quite a different direction if we break the sentence after 'you', so that 'know' lacks a grammatical subject, suggesting both an elision ('I know') and an imperative ('one must know'). This is followed by an undecidable 'it', which makes something happen whose effects are ongoing, as indicated by the present perfect tense. Finally, the closing of her eyes participates in the sentence's ambivalence by suggesting pleasure, bore-dom, and even forbearance, in addition to the imminent death of this memory itself. Bursting at the seams, the sentence mirrors the father's stomach and the lover's abdomen dissolving into each other: something is about to give.

The sexual intimacy that emerges as a rearrangement of the sitting position – from the ledge to face to face – remains utterly ambivalent too: they are 'closed' in themselves, in an image in which the modesty is gestural but not linguistic. *Company* is fearlessly experimental in the treatment of a familiar heterosexual encounter: it skirts close to the sentimental as the register of memory, rejects sentimentality's implicit denial of hate by queering time, stages the uneasy proximity between the memory of one's father and the presence of one's lover, and formally strains against its own unbuttoned waistband. *Company* resists any 'redemptive perversion': it performs a systolic/diastolic movement between tender recollection and dissection, 'credence' and 'incontrovertibility': both are on a knife edge, neither denies the other.

4 Conclusion

Willie feels 'fucked up', not 'sucked up'. His surprise is at the s.

(Beckett, 2014, 429)

'se tenir coït' does not exist. If it did it could only mean 'fuck oneself'. Hence Hamm's alarm, for if the flea were fucking itself more fleas might be expected. You should also note that 'baiser' is the slang for 'fuck' … I hope this is now as clear as semen.

(Beckett, 2014, 185)

---

[13] Beckett, MS12-3–4, fol. 11r, reads: 'She too did you but know it has closed her eyes' (Boston College Libraries, Boston, Massachusetts) and so does UoR MS1765, fol. 02r (Beckett International Foundation, University of Reading). Beckett, UoR MS1822, fol. 18r reads: 'Did you but know it she too has closed her eyes' (Beckett International Foundation, University of Reading). 'Heard in the Dark 2' (Beckett, 1979, 3) corroborates the 'it' variant. Dirk Van Hulle, private communication, September 2022. See Beckett (2024).

'Sexuality should be treated with special respect in times of great social stress', wrote Gayle S. Rubin in 1984. At a historical moment when the question of politics is at the centre of literary and cultural debates, this Element has addressed contemporary preoccupations with gender and sexuality in Beckett studies. If there is a 'special respect' towards gender and sexuality in Beckett, it is because they are treated not as solemn issues but as engines powering the comedy of his tragic work.

Recent scholarship has been invaluable in recuperating the more historically relevant political aspects of the Beckett oeuvre, despite the occasional temptation to overstate the work's relation to specific political projects (Morin, 2017; McNaughton, 2018; Davis and Bailey, 2020; Kennedy, 2020). The episode which perhaps best captures the relation between Beckett and politics is an early one, which leads us back to Nancy Cunard (discussed in Section 2.1). In 1937 she circulated a political questionnaire, which asked writers to state their position regarding the Spanish Civil War in a pamphlet published by the *Left Review*. It stated: 'It is clear to many of us throughout the whole world that now, as certainly never before, we are determined or compelled, to take sides. The equivocal attitude, the Ivory Tower, the paradoxical, the ironic detachment, will no longer do' (Cunard, 1937). The 148 responses were classified as 'For the Republic, against Franco and Fascism' (127), 'Neutral' (16) and 'Pro-Franco and Pro-Fascism' (5). Beckett's response (filed under the first category) stood out not just from the equivocating Eliot and the predictably hectoring Pound but also from the commitment displayed by W. H. Auden, Rebecca West, and Sylvia Townsend Warner. His funny one-liner – '¡UPTHEREPUBLIC!' – with its homage to Spanish punctuation, encapsulated the complex relation between politics and culture, made its readers vacillate in their potential self-righteousness, resisted being co-opted, and refused to sit on the fence.[14]

Things are more complicated when we look at the politics of gender and sexuality. Unsurprisingly, no one has agitated for a feminist Beckett or recruited Beckett to queer as an identity. Neither has this Element, which has taken a non-essentialist approach to demonstrate that feminist and queer theory can account for the work's need to be 'on the lookout for an elsewhere'. A perspective which estranged the assumed common sense of the straight critical mind made it possible to reconsider questions of literary tradition and periodisation (the role of decadence and race relations in the early poetry; the relation between *All Strange Away* and 'Nighttown'); aesthetics (*L'image* and *How It Is*); material presence on stage (the *Texts for Nothing* and their 2016 adaptation); gender

---

[14] By repeating 'up the republic!' *Malone Dies* revisits the question of political rightfulness.

and sexual politics ('Moly', *Not I*, *Dream*); and disturbing attachments (the Mitchell correspondence, *Company*).

Building on feminist, queer, and trans theory, *Insufferable: Beckett, Gender and Sexuality* has extended the conversation in two directions. After establishing how Beckett's work contributed to the origin of the 'antisocial thesis' in queer studies, it has asked, after Kadji Amin, 'why are we under the impression that queer scholarship should have queer objects? (Amin, 2016, 101). An engagement with the history of feminism and sexuality studies and its latest theoretical developments can make us understand aspects of the work previously overlooked, underplayed, and misinterpreted: this Element is the first step in that direction. The temporal arc covered in this Element maps key debates ranging from gender essentialism to sexual politics and from sexuality studies to queer and trans theory. As the intransitive title of this Element implies, the Beckett oeuvre punctures the self-righteousness of any project of sexual liberation and progressive sexual politics: the connection between experimental language and perceived sexual impropriety does not happen in the name of transgressive politics or naïve belief in the redemptive power of sex. By discouraging celebration or redemption, the Beckett oeuvre makes our critical faltering instructive, and pleasurable.

This Element has shown that Beckett's work is attached to sexuality as temporarily consolatory but ultimately unbearable, committed to the estrangement of sexual aims and objects, able to question the relations between gender and identity, and fearless in its exploration of the proximity between familial and sexual love. The politics of gender and sexuality make us see an unfamiliar Beckett, harder to idealise but no less compelling.

References

Ahmed, Sara (2010), 'Killing Joy: Feminism and the History of Happiness', *Signs*, 35:3, pp. 571–94.

Albright, Daniel (2003), *Beckett and Aesthetics*, Cambridge: Cambridge University Press.

Althusser, Louis (1964), 'Marxism and Humanism', *Cahiers de l'I.S.E.A.*, June. www.marxists.org/reference/archive/althusser/index.htm.

Amin, Kadji (2016), 'Against Queer Objects', *Feminist Formations*, 28:2, pp. 101–11.

Amin, Kadji (2017), *Disturbing Attachments*, Durham, NC: Duke University Press.

Barnett, Anthony (2007), *Listening for Henry Crowder: A Monograph on His almost Lost Music, with the Poems and Music of Henry Music*, Lewes: AB Faber and Allardyce Books.

Baroghel, Elsa (2017), 'Samuel Beckett, lecteur de Sade: *Comment C'est* et *Les 120 Journées de Sodome*', in Llewellyn Brown (ed.), *La violence dans l'œuvre de Samuel Beckett: entre langage et corps*, 'Samuel Beckett', vol. 4, Paris: Lettres Modernes Minard/Classiques Garnier, pp. 227–59.

Baroghel, Elsa (2018), 'Beckett, with Sade: Sadean Intertexts and Aesthetics in Samuel Beckett's Work', unpublished doctoral thesis, New College, University of Oxford.

Baroghel, Elsa (2022), 'How It Was in Silling: *Comment c'est* and *Les 120 journées de Sodome*: An Intertextual Case Study', *Journal of Beckett Studies*, 31:1, pp. 80–94.

Barolini, Teodolinda (2014–20), The Divine Comedy *by Dante Alighieri*, Digital Dante edition with Commento Baroliniano (Columbia University). https://digitaldante.columbia.edu/dante/divine-comedy/paradiso/paradiso-9.

Barry, Elizabeth, Ulrika Maude and Laura Salisbury (2016), 'Introduction: Beckett, Medicine and the Brain', *Journal of Medical Humanities*, 37:2, pp. 127–35.

Barthes, Roland ([1977] 2022), *Fragments of a Lover's Discourse*, London: Vintage.

Beckett, Samuel, *Whoroscope Notebook*, UoR MS3000, Beckett International Foundation, University of Reading.

Beckett, Samuel, Correspondence with Pamela Mitchell, UoR MS5060, Beckett International Foundation, University of Reading.

Beckett, Samuel (1931), 'Yoke of Liberty', in Samuel Putnam (ed.), *The European Caravan: A Critical Anthology of the New Spirit in European Literature*, New York: Brewer, Warren and Putnam, p. 480.

Beckett, Samuel (1959), 'L'image', *X: A Quarterly Review*, 1:1, pp. 35–7.

Beckett, Samuel (1960), Original Manuscript of *Play Female Solo*, UoR MS1227, Beckett International Foundation, University of Reading.

Beckett, Samuel (1961), *Comment c'est*, Paris: Les Éditions de Minuit.

Beckett, Samuel (1972), *Têtes-mortes*, Paris: Les Éditions de Minuit.

Beckett, Samuel (1975), *No's Knife: Collected Shorter Prose 1945–1966*, London: Calder & Boyars.

Beckett, Samuel (1979), *Heard in the Dark 2*, ed. John Pilling, *Journal of Beckett Studies*, 5, pp. 7–8.

Beckett, Samuel (1981), *Mal vu mal dit*, Paris: Les Éditions de Minuit.

Beckett, Samuel (1985), *Compagnie*, Paris: Les Éditions de Minuit.

Beckett, Samuel (1992), *Quad et autres pieces pour la télévision*, suivi de *L'épuisé* par *Gilles* Deleuze, Paris: Les Éditions de Minuit.

Beckett, Samuel (1993), *Dream of Fair to Middling Women*, New York: Arcade.

Beckett, Samuel (1995), *The Complete Short Prose, 1929–1989*, ed. S. E. Gontarski, New York: Grove Press.

Beckett, Samuel (1998), *No Author Better Served: The Correspondence of Samuel Beckett and Alan Schneider*, ed. Maurice Harmon, Cambridge, MA: Harvard University Press.

Beckett, Samuel (2003), 'Annotations of *Dream of Fair to Middling Women*, ed. John Pilling', *Journal of Beckett Studies*, 12:1 and 2.

Beckett, Samuel (2006), *The Complete Dramatic Works*, London: Faber and Faber.

Beckett, Samuel (2009a), *Company, Ill Seen Ill Said, Worstward Ho, Stirrings Still*, ed. Dirk Van Hulle, London: Faber and Faber.

Beckett, Samuel (2009b), *How It Is*, ed. Éduard Magessa O'Reilly, London: Faber and Faber.

Beckett, Samuel (2009c), *The Letters of Samuel Beckett, Vol. I: 1929–1940*, ed. Martha Dow Fehsenfeld and Lois More Overbeck, Cambridge: Cambridge University Press.

Beckett, Samuel (2009d), *Molloy*, ed. Shane Weller, London: Faber and Faber.

Beckett, Samuel (2009e), *Murphy*, ed. J. C. C. Mays, London: Faber and Faber.

Beckett, Samuel (2010a), *Malone Dies*, ed. Peter Boxall, London: Faber and Faber.

Beckett, Samuel (2010b), *Texts for Nothing and Other Shorter Prose 1950–1976*, ed. Mark Nixon, London: Faber and Faber.

Beckett, Samuel (2010c), *The Unnamable*, ed. Steven Connor, London: Faber and Faber.

Beckett, Samuel (2011), *The Letters of Samuel Beckett, Vol. II: 1941–1956*, ed. George Craig, Martha Dow Fehsenfeld, Dan Gunn and Lois More Overbeck, Cambridge: Cambridge University Press.

Beckett, Samuel (2012), *Collected Poems*, ed. Seán Lawlor and John Pilling, London: Faber and Faber.

Beckett, Samuel (2014), *The Letters of Samuel Beckett, Vol. III: 1957–1965*, ed. George Craig, Martha Dow Fehsenfeld, Dan Gunn and Lois More Overbeck, Cambridge: Cambridge University Press.

Beckett, Samuel (2016), *The Letters of Samuel Beckett, Vol. IV: 1966–1989*, ed. George Craig, Martha Dow Fehsenfeld, Dan Gunn and Lois More Overbeck, Cambridge: Cambridge University Press.

Beckett, Samuel (2024), *Company / Compagnie*: a digital genetic edition (Series 'The Beckett Digital Manuscript Project', module 9), edited by Georgina Nugent and Vincent Neyt, Brussels: University Press Antwerp (ASP/UPA), www.beckettarchive.org.

Ben-Zvi, Linda (1990), *Women in Beckett: Performance and Critical Perspectives*, Champaign: University of Illinois Press.

Berlant, Lauren (1997), *The Queen of American Goes to Washington* City, Durham, NC: Duke University Press.

Berlant, Lauren (2000), *Intimacy*, Chicago, IL: University of Chicago Press.

Berlant, Lauren (2008), *The Female Complaint: The Unfinished Business of Sentimentality in American Culture*, Durham, NC: Duke University Press.

Berlant, Lauren and Lee Edelman (2014), *Sex, Or the Unbearable*, Durham, NC: Duke University Press.

Bersani, Leo (1976), *A Future for Astyanax*, Boston, MA: Little, Brown.

Bersani, Leo (1986), *The Freudian Body: Psychoanalysis and Art*, New York: Columbia University Press.

Bersani, Leo (1987), 'Is the Rectum a Grave?', *October AIDS: Cultural Analysis/Cultural Activism*, 43, pp. 197–222.

Bersani, Leo (1995), *Homos*, Cambridge, MA: Harvard University Press.

Bersani, Leo (2000), 'Sociality and Sexuality', *Critical Enquiry*, 26:4, pp. 641–56.

Bersani, Leo (2018), *Receptive Bodies*, Chicago, IL: University of Chicago Press.

Bersani, Leo and Ulysse Dutoit (1993), *Arts of Impoverishment*: *Beckett, Rothko, Resnais*, Cambridge, MA: Harvard University Press.

Billington, Michael (2016), 'No's Knife Review. Lisa Dwan Excels in Beckett's Strange No Man's Land', *The Guardian*, 4 October.

Blanchot, Maurice (2003), *The Book to Come*, trans. Charlotte Mandell, Stanford, CA: Stanford University Press.

Blanchot, Maurice (2004), *Lautremont and Sade*, trans. Stuart Kendall and Michelle Kendall, Stanford, CA: Stanford University Press.

Bond Stockton, Kathryn (2009), *The Queer Child, or Growing Sideways in the Twentieth Century*, Durham, NC: Duke University Press.

Boxall, Peter (2004), 'Beckett and Homoeroticism', in Lois Oppenheim (ed.), *Palgrave Advances in Samuel Beckett Studies*, Basingstoke: Palgrave MacMillan, pp. 110–32.

Brater, Enoch (1994), *The Drama in the Text: Beckett's Late Fiction*, Oxford: Oxford University Press.

Brim, Matt (2020), *Poor Queer Studies: Confronting Elitism in the University*, Durham, NC: Duke University Press.

Brown, Llewellyn (2018), *"Textes pour rien"/"Texts for Nothing" de Samuel Beckett. Le corps de la voix impossible*, Série Samuel Beckett, 6, Paris: Classiques Garnier, Lettres modernes Minard.

Brown, Llewellyn (2019), *Beckett, Lacan, and the Gaze*, Stuttgart: Ibidem Press.

Brown, Wendy (1993), 'Wounded Attachments', *Political Theory*, 21:3, pp. 390–410.

Bryden, Mary (1993), *Women in Samuel Beckett's Prose and Drama: Her Own Other*, Basingstoke: Macmillan.

Butler, Judith ([1990] 1999), *Gender Trouble*, London: Routledge.

Butler, Judith (1993), *Bodies That Matter. On the Discursive Limits of 'Sex'*, London: Routledge.

Butler, Judith (1997), *Excitable Speech: A Politics of the Performative*, London: Routledge.

Buse, Peter and Rob Lapsley (2023), 'Gaps in Transmission: Reading Lacan's *Télévision'*, *Modern Philology*, 120:3, pp. 394–415.

Carville, Conor (2018), *Samuel Beckett and the Visual Arts*, Cambridge: Cambridge University Press.

Caselli, Daniela (2005a), *Beckett's Dantes: Intertextuality in the Fiction and Criticism*, Manchester: Manchester University Press.

Caselli, Daniela (2005b), 'The Child in Beckett' and 'Tiny Little Things in Beckett's *Company'*, *Samuel Beckett Today/Aujourd'hui*, 15, pp. 259–60 and pp. 271–80.

Caselli, Daniela, ed. (2010), *Beckett and Nothing: Trying to Understand Beckett*, Manchester: Manchester University Press.

Caselli, Daniela (2012), 'Beckett and Leopardi', in S. E. Gontarski (ed.), *The Beckett Critical* Reader, Edinburgh: Edinburgh University Press, pp. 135–51.

Caselli, Daniela (2020), 'Address', *The Beckett Circle*, https://samuelbeckettso ciety.org/beckettcircle.

Caselli, Daniela, Steven Connor and Laura Salisbury, eds (2001/2), *Other Becketts*, special double issue *Journal of Beckett Studies*, 10:1–2.

Chattopadhay, Arka (2018), *Beckett, Lacan, and the Mathematical Writing of the Real*, London: Bloomsbury Academic.

Clark, Suzanne (1991), *Sentimental Modernism: Women Writers and the Revolution of the World*, Bloomington: Indiana University Press.

Cohn, Ruby (2005), *A Beckett Canon*, Ann Arbor: University of Michigan Press.

Crowder, Henry (1930), *Henry Music*, Paris: The Hours Press.

Crowder, Henry with Hugo Speck (1987), *As Wonderful As All That? Henry Crowder's Memoir of His Affair with Nancy Cunard 1928–1935*, with an introduction and epilogue by Robert L. Allen, Navarro, CA: Wild Trees Press.

Cunard, Nancy (1934), *Negro Anthology*, London: Wishart.

Cunard, Nancy (1937), 'Authors Take Sides on the Spanish Civil War', *Left Review*, https://tinyurl.com/4zfypr44.

Cunningham, David (2005), 'Asceticism Against Colour, or Modernism, Abstraction and the Lateness of Beckett', *New Formations*, 55, pp. 104–19.

Cunningham, David (2008), '"We Have Our Being in Justice": Formalism, Abstraction and Beckett's "Ethics"', in Russell Smith (ed.), *Beckett and Ethics*, London: Continuum, pp. 21–37.

Davis, William and Helen Bailey, eds (2020), *Beckett and Politics*, Basingstoke: Palgrave Macmillan.

Deleuze, Gilles and Felix Guattari (1975), *Kafka: pour une littérature mineure*, Paris: Les Éditions de Minuit.

Deleuze, Gilles and Félix Guattari (1983), 'What Is a Minor Literature?', *Mississippi Review*, 11:3, pp. 13–33.

Derrida, Jacques (1992), '"This Strange Institution Called Literature': An Interview with Jacques Derrida', trans. Geoffrey Bennington and Rachel Bowlby, in *Acts of Literature*, ed. Derek Attridge, New York: Routledge, pp. 60–1.

de Beauvoir, Simone (1953), *Must we Burn Sade?*, trans. Annette Michelson, bibliography and chronology compiled by Paul Dinnage, London: Peter Neville.

de Beauvoir, Simone ([1949] 2010), *The Second Sex*, trans. Constance Borde and Sheila Malovaney-Chevallier, London: Vintage.

de Berg, Jean ([1956] 1966), *The Image*, trans. Patsy Southgate, preface by Pauline Réage, New York: Grove Press.

Dinshaw, Carolyn (2012), *How Soon Is Now? Medieval Texts, Amateur Readers and the Queerness of Time*, Durham, NC: Duke University Press.

Dinshaw, Carolyn (2019), 'Afterlives', *GLQ*, 25:1, pp. 5–6.

Dolar, Mladen (2010), 'Nothing Has Changed', in Daniela Caselli (ed.), *Beckett and Nothing*, Manchester: Manchester University Press, pp. 48–64.

DuBois, W. E. B. ([1903] 2018), *The Souls of Black Folk: Essays and Sketches*, Amherst: University of Massachusetts Press.

Duggan, Lisa (2002), 'The New Homonormativity: The Sexual Politics of Neoliberalism', in Russ Castronovo and Dana D. Nelson (eds),

Materializing Democracy: Toward a Revitalized Cultural Politics, Durham, NC: Duke University Press, pp. 175–94.

Edelman, Lee (2004), *No Future: Queer Theory and the Death Drive*, Durham, NC: Duke University Press.

Eng, David L. with Judith Halberstam and José Esteban Muñoz (2005), 'Introduction', *What's Queer about Queer Studies Now? Social Text* special issue, 23:3–4, pp. 1–17.

Feldman, Matthew (2006), *Beckett's Books: A Cultural History of Samuel Beckett's 'Interwar Notes'*, London: Bloomsbury Academic.

Fifield, Peter (2014), '"I Am Writing a Manifesto Because I Have Nothing to Say," Samuel Beckett and the Interwar Avant-Garde', in S. E. Gontarski (ed.), *The Edinburgh Companion to Samuel Beckett and the Arts*, Edinburgh: Edinburgh University Press, pp. 170–84.

Foster, Roy (2011), 'Darkness and Kindness', *The New Republic*, 23 November.

Fox, Pamela (1994), *Class Fictions: Shame and Resistance in the British Working-Class Novel, 1890–1945*, Durham, NC: Duke University Press.

Fraser, Graham (1995), 'The Pornographic Imagination in *All Strange Away*', *Modern Fiction Studies*, 41:3–4, pp. 515–30.

Freeman, Elizabeth, ed. (2007), *Queer Temporalities*, special issue of *GLQ*, 13:2–3.

Freud, Sigmund ([1920] 2001), 'Beyond the Pleasure Principle' (1920), in *The Standard Edition of the Complete Psychological Works*, trans. and general ed. James Strachey in collaboration with Anna Freud, assisted by Alix Strachey and Alan Tyson, vol. XVIII 1920–2, London: Vintage, pp. 7–64.

Friedman, Alan Warren (2000), *Beckett in Black and Red: The Translations of Nancy Cunard's "Negro" (1934)*, Lexington: University Press of Kentucky.

Friedman, Alan Warren (2018), *Surreal Beckett: Samuel Beckett, James Joyce and Surrealism*, New York: Routledge.

Friedman, Melvin J. (1960), 'Samuel Beckett and the "Nouveau Roman"', *Wisconsin Studies in Contemporary Literature*, 1:2, pp. 22–36.

Gabriel, Kay (2020), 'Gender As Accumulation Strategy', *Invert*, 1, invertjournal.org.uk.

Gavin, Gareth (2022), 'A Self-Made Man?', *Prototype*, 4, pp. 99–105.

Gontarski, S. E. (1995), 'Introduction', in Samuel Beckett: *The Complete Short Prose, 1929–1989*, ed. S. E. Gontarski, New York, Grove Press, pp. xi–xxxii.

Gontarski, S. E. (2006), 'Greying the Canon: Beckett in Performance, Beckett Performing', in S. E. Gontarski and Anthony Uhlmann (eds), *Beckett after Beckett*, Gainsville: University Press of Florida, pp. 141–57. Reprinted in S. E. Gontarski (2017), *Beckett Matters*, Edinburgh: Edinburgh University Press, pp. 240–54.

Gopal, Priyamvada (2019), *Insurgent Empire: Anticolonial Resistance and British Dissent*, London: Verso.

Green, Eleanor (2022), 'Queer Sexuality in Samuel Beckett's Late Prose', unpublished doctoral thesis, University of Manchester.

Gussow, Mel (1997), 'When Beckett Decided He'd Fix the Record', *New York Times*, 4 January.

Jagose, Annamarie (2015), 'The Trouble with Antinormativity', *differences: A Journal of Feminist Cultural Studies*, 26:1, pp. 26–47.

Joyce, James ([1922] 2008), *Ulysses. The 1922 Text*, introduction by Jeri Johnson, Oxford: Oxford University Press.

Juliet, Charles (1986), *Rencontre avec Samuel Beckett*, Paris: Éditions Fata Morgana.

Halberstam, Jack (2011), *The Queer Art of Failure*, Durham, NC: Duke University Press.

Hall, Donald E. and Annamarie Jagose with Andrea Bebell and Susan Potter, eds (2013), *The Routledge Queer Studies Reader*, New York: Routledge.

Hansford, James (1983), 'Skullscapes: Imaginative Strategies in the Later Prose of Samuel Beckett', unpublished doctoral thesis, University of Reading.

Hartman, Saidiya V. (1997), *Scenes of Subjection: Terror, Slavery, and Self-Making in Nineteenth-Century America*, Oxford: Oxford University Press.

Hartman, Saidiya V. (2007), *Lose Your Mother: A Journey along the Atlantic Slave Route*, Basingstoke: Palgrave Macmillan.

Hartman, Saidiya V. and Frank B. Wilderson III (2003), 'The Position of the Unthought: An Interview with Saidiya V. Hartman conducted by Frank B. Wilderson III", *Qui parle*, 13:2, pp. 183–201.

Keeling, Kara (2019), *Black Times, Queer Futures*, New York: New York University Press.

Keller, John Robert (2002), *Samuel Beckett and the Primacy of Love*, Manchester: Manchester University Press.

Kennedy, Seán (2010), *Beckett and Ireland*, Cambridge: Cambridge University Press.

Kennedy, Seán (2020), *Beckett beyond the Normal*, Edinburgh: Edinburgh University Press.

Kenner, Hugh (1978), *Joyce's Voices*, Berkeley: University of California Press.

Klossowski, Pierre (1991), *Sade My Neighbour*, trans. with an introduction by Alphonso Lingis, Evanston, IL: Northwestern University Press.

Knowlson, James (1996), *Damned to Fame: The Life of Samuel Beckett*, London: Bloomsbury.

Krimper, Michael, ed. (2022), *Journal of Beckett Studies, Dossier: Beckett's Translations of Sade for* Transition, 31:1.

Lacan, Jacques (2015), 'Freud Forever: An Interview with Panorama', trans. Philip Dravers, *Hurly-Burly: The International Lacanian Journal of Psychoanalysis*, 12, pp. 13–22.

Laplanche, Jean (1976), *Life and Death in Psychoanalysis*, trans. with an introduction by Jeffrey Mehlman, Baltimore, MD: Johns Hopkins University Press.

Lesnik-Oberstein, Karín (2017), 'The Object of Neuroscience and Literary Studies', *Textual Practice*, 31:7, pp. 1315–31.

Long Chu, Andrea (2019), *Females*, London: Verso.

Lorde, Audre ([1984] 2019), *Sister Outsider*, Harmondsworth: Penguin.

Marcuse, Herbert ([1964] 2007), *One-Dimensional Man: Studies in the Ideology of Advanced Industrial Society*, London: Routledge.

Marder, Elissa (2016), 'Inhuman Beauty: Baudelaire's Bad Sex', *differences: A Journal of Feminist Cultural Studies*, 27:1, pp. 1–24.

Maude, Ulrika and Matthew Feldman, eds (2009), *Beckett and Phenomenology*, London: Bloomsbury Continuum.

McKeon, Belinda (2016), 'Lisa Dwan: Beckett Made These Wounds Universal', *The Guardian*, 17 September.

McMullan, Anna (1993), *Theatre on Trial: Samuel Beckett's Later Drama*, London: Routledge.

McMullan, Anna (2010), *Performing Embodiment in Samuel Beckett's Drama*, New York: Routledge.

McNaughton, James (2018), *Beckett and the Politics of the Aftermath*, Oxford: Oxford University Press.

McTighe, Trish (2019), 'Everyday Catastrophe: Gender, Labour and Power in Beckett's Theatre', *Journal of Beckett Studies*, 28:1, pp. 19–34.

Millett, Kate ([1970] 1999), *Sexual Politics*, London: Virago.

Miller, Monica L. (2009), *Slaves to Fashion: Black Dandyism and the Styling of Black Diasporic Identity*, Durham, NC: Duke University Press.

Mills, Robert (2018), *Derek Jarman's Medieval Modern*, Rochester: Boydell and Brewer.

Mitchell, Pamela (*c*.1953–70), 'Correspondence with Samuel Beckett', UoR MS5060, Beckett International Foundation, University of Reading.

Morin, Emily (2017), *Beckett's Political Imagination*, Cambridge: Cambridge University Press.

Morrison, Toni (1992), *Playing in the Dark: Whiteness and the Literary Imagination*, Harvard, MA: Harvard University Press.

Nayak, Suryia (2014), *Race, Gender and the Activism of Black Feminist Theory: Working with Audre Lorde*, London: Routledge.

Ngai, Sianne (2005), *Ugly Feelings*, Cambridge, MA: Harvard University Press.

Nietzsche, Friedrich ([1886] 1973), *Beyond Good and Evil*, trans. R. J. Hollingdale, New York: Penguin.

Nixon, Mark (2010), 'Preface', in Samuel Beckett: *Texts for Nothing and other Shorter Prose, 1950–1976*, ed. Mark Nixon, London: Faber and Faber, pp. vii–xxiv.

Periyan, Natasha (2018), *The Politics of 1930s British Literature: Education, Gender and Class*, London: Bloomsbury.

Piette, Adam (2011), 'Beckett, Affect and the Face', *Textual Practice*, 25:2, pp. 281–95.

Pilling, John (2006), *A Samuel Beckett Chronology*, Basingstoke: Palgrave Macmillan.

Pilling, John (2012), 'No Lack of Void: Review of *The Letters of Samuel Beckett 1941–1956*', *Journal of Beckett Studies*, 21:1, pp. 106–21.

Pilling, John (2014), 'Beckett/Sade: Texts for Nothing', in S. E. Gontarski (ed.), *The Edinburgh Companion to Samuel Beckett and the Arts*, Edinburgh: Edinburgh University Press, pp. 117–30.

Pinget, Robert (1961), *Clope au dossier*, Paris: Éditions de Minuit.

Praz, Mario [1930] (2008), *La carne, la morte e il diavolo nella letteratura romantica*. Milan: Rizzoli.

Preciado, Paul B. (2018), *Countersexual Manifesto*, trans. Kevin Jerry Dunn with a preface by Jack Halberstam, New York: Columbia University Press.

Rabaté, Jean-Michel (2020), *Beckett and Sade*, Cambridge: Cambridge University Press.

Radway, Janice (1984), *Reading the Romance: Women, Patriarchy, and Popular Literature*, Chapel Hill: University of North Carolina Press.

Ravez, Stéphanie (2001), 'From Cithera to Philautia: An Excursion into Beckettian Love', *Journal of Beckett Studies*, 10:1–2, pp. 136–51.

Roof, Judith (2002), 'Is There Sex after Gender? Ungendering/*The Unnamable*', *Journal of the Midwest Modern Language Association*, 35:1, pp. 50–67.

Rose, Jacqueline [1986] (2020), *Sexuality in the Field of Vision*, London: Verso.

Rose, Jacqueline (1991), *The Haunting of Sylvia Plath*, London: Virago.

Rubin, Gayle ([1975 and 1984] 2012), 'The Traffic in Women: Notes on the Political Economy of Sex' and 'Thinking Sex: Notes for a Radical Theory of the Politics of Sexuality', in *Deviations: A Gayle Rubin Reader*, Durham, NC: Duke University Press, pp. 33–65 and 137–81.

Salisbury, Laura (2010), '"Something or Nothing": Beckett and the Matter of Language', in Daniela Caselli (ed.), *Beckett and Nothing: Trying to Understand Beckett*, Manchester: Manchester University Press, pp. 213–36.

Salisbury, Laura (2011), 'Bulimic Beckett: Food for Thought and the Archive of Analysis', *Critical Quarterly*, 3:53, pp. 60–80.

Salisbury, Laura (2012), *Samuel Beckett: Laughing Matters, Comic Timing*, Edinburgh: Edinburgh University Press.

Salisbury, Laura (2016), 'Jackson's Parrot: Samuel Beckett, Aphasic Speech Automatisms, and Psychosomatic Language', *Journal of Medical Humanities*, 37, pp. 205–22.

Salisbury, Laura (2017), '"I Switch Off": Beckett, Bion, and Thinking in Torturous Times', *Samuel Beckett Today/Aujourd'hui*, 29:2, pp. 51–65.

Salisbury, Laura (2023), 'Slow Violence and Slow Going: Encountering Beckett in a Time of Climate Catastrophe', in Michiko Tsushima, Yoshiki Tajiri and Mariko Hori Tanaka (eds), *Samuel Beckett and Catastrophe*, Basingstoke: Palgrave Macmillan.

Salisbury, Laura and Andrew Shail, eds (2010), *Neurology and Modernity: A Cultural History of Nervous Systems 1800–1950*, Basingstoke: Palgrave Macmillan.

Sartre, Jean-Paul (1960), *Critique de la raison dialectique*, vol. I, Paris: Gallimard.

Sedgwick, Eve Kosofsky (1990), *Epistemology of the Closet*, Berkeley: University of California Press.

Sedgwick, Eve Kosofsky, ed. (1997), *Novel Gazing: Queer Readings in Fiction*, Durham, NC: Duke University Press.

Sharpe, Christina (2016), *In the Wake: On Blackness and Being*, Durham, NC: Duke University Press.

Sheehan, Paul (2006), 'Births for Nothing: Beckett's Ontology of Parturition', in Anthony Uhlmann and S. E. Gontarski (eds), *Beckett after Beckett*, Tallahassee: University of Florida Press, pp. 177–86.

Sherry, Vincent (2014), *Modernism and the Reinvention of Decadence*, Cambridge: Cambridge University Press.

Simpson, Hannah (2020), '"He Wants to Know if It Hurts!" Suffering beyond Redemption in *Waiting for Godot*', in Seán Kennedy (ed.), *Beckett beyond the Normal*, Edinburgh: Edinburgh University Press, pp. 79–89.

Simpson, Hannah (2022a), '"In Control ... under Control": *Not I*, Sexual Trauma, and Rape Play', *Samuel Beckett Today/Aujourd'hui*, 34:1, pp. 24–38.

Simpson, Hannah (2022b), *Samuel Beckett and Disability Performance*, Basingstoke: Palgrave Macmillan.

Smith, Molly and Juno Mac (2018), *Revolting Prostitutes: The Fight for Sex Workers' Rights*, London: Verso.

Sontag, Susan (1967), 'The Pornographic Imagination', *Partisan Review*, 34:2, pp. 181–212.

Spillers, Hortense J. (1987), 'Mama's Baby, Papa's Maybe: An American Grammar', *Diacritics*, 17:2, pp. 64–81.

Stacey, Jackie (2015), 'Crossing over with Tilda Swinton: The Mistress of "Flat Affect"', *International Journal of Politics, Culture, and Society*, 28:3, pp. 243–71.

Stacey, Jackie (2019), 'Butch Noir', *differences: A Journal of Feminist Cultural Studies*, 30:2, pp. 30–71.

Stewart, Paul (2011), *Sex and Aesthetics in Samuel Beckett's Work*, Basingstoke: Palgrave MacMillan.

Thomas, Calvin (2019), 'Beckett's Queer Art of Failure', in Jean-Michel Rabaté (ed.), *The New Samuel Beckett Studies*, Cambridge: Cambridge University Press, pp. 157–74.

Thomson, Stephen (2010), '"A Tangle of Tatters": Ghosts and the Busy Nothing in *Footfalls*', in Daniela Caselli (ed.), *Beckett and Nothing: Trying to Understand Beckett*, Manchester: Manchester University Press, pp. 65–83.

Tranter, Rhys (2013), 'The Dan Gunn Interview', *Quarterly Conversation*, 4 March, https://quarterlyconversation.com.

Uhlmann, Anthony (2006), *Beckett and the Philosophical Image*, Cambridge: Cambridge University Press.

Van Hulle, Dirk and Mark Nixon (2013), *Samuel Beckett's Library*, Cambridge: Cambridge University Press.

Vincent, Glyn (2011), 'What's So Secret about Samuel Beckett', *Huffington Post*, 1 November.

Walker, Dominic (2020), 'Beckett's Safe Words: Normalising Torture in *How It Is*', in Seán Kennedy (ed.), *Beckett beyond the Normal*, Edinburgh: Edinburgh University Press, pp. 117–32.

Walton, Jean (2010), 'Modernity and the Peristaltic Subject', in Laura Salisbury and Andrew Shail (eds), *Neurology and Modernity: A Cultural History of Nervous Systems, 1800–1950*, Basingstoke: Palgrave Macmillan, pp. 245–66.

Weiss, Katherine (2021), '"Of her tenacious trace": Samuel Beckett and Contemporary Art', *Journal of Beckett Studies*, 30:2, pp. 174–87.

Weller, Shane (2006), 'When the Other Comes Too Close: Derrida and the Threat of Affinity', *Kritikos* 3.

Weller, Shane (2008), 'The Anethics of Desire: Beckett, Racine, Sade', in Russell Smith (ed.), *Beckett and Ethics*, London: Continuum, pp. 102–17.

West, Cornel (2020), Interview with Anderson Cooper, www.youtube.com/watch?v=90G_QdxqqJs, mins 5.50 to 6.15.

West, Paul (1983/4), 'Deciphering a Beckett Fiction on His Birthday', *Parnassus: Poetry in Review*, 11:2, pp. 319–22.

Wiegman, Robyn and Elizabeth Wilson (2015), 'Introduction: Antinormativity's Queer Conventions', *differences: A Journal of Feminist Cultural Studies*, 26:1, pp. 1–25.

Wiegman, Robyn (2017), 'Sex and Negativity; or, What Queer Theory Has for You', *Cultural Critique*, 95, pp. 219–43.

Wimbush, Andy (2018), '"Omniscience and Omnipotence": *Molloy* and the End of "Joyceology"', in Olga Beloborodova, Dirk Van Hulle and Pim Verhulst (eds), *Beckett and Modernism*, Basingstoke: Palgrave Macmillan, pp. 95–105.

Winnicott, Donald (1949), 'Hate in the Counter-Transference', *International Journal of Psychoanalysis*, 30, pp. 69–74.

Winstanley, A. M. (2013), '"First Dirty, Then Make Clean": Samuel Beckett's Peristaltic Modernism, 1932–1958', unpublished doctoral thesis, University of York.

Wolff, Janet (2008), *The Aesthetics of Uncertainty*, New York: Columbia University Press.

Woodworth, Robert S. ([1931] 1965), *Contemporary Schools of Psychology*, London: Methuen and Company.

Acknowledgements

Jackie Stacey, Monica Pearl, Janet Wolff, Dharmakārunyā Tidd, Eleanor Green, Suryia Nayak, Peter Buse, Erica Burman, Karín Lesnik-Oberstein, Gareth Gavin and Ben Harker: thank you.

For Ale

Cambridge Elements ≡

Beckett Studies

Dirk Van Hulle
University of Oxford

Dirk Van Hulle is Professor of Bibliography and Modern Book History at the University of Oxford and director of the Centre for Manuscript Genetics at the University of Antwerp.

Mark Nixon
University of Reading

Mark Nixon is Professor in Modern Literature at the University of Reading and the Co-Director of the Beckett International Foundation.

About the Series

This series presents cutting-edge research by distinguished and emerging scholars, providing space for the most relevant debates informing Beckett studies as well as neglected aspects of his work. In times of technological development, religious radicalism, unprecedented migration, gender fluidity, environmental and social crisis, Beckett's works find increased resonance. Cambridge Elements in Beckett Studies is a key resource for readers interested in the current state of the field.

Cambridge Elements ☰

Beckett Studies

Elements in the Series

Experimental Beckett: Contemporary Performance Practices
Nicholas E. Johnson and Jonathan Heron

Postcognitivist Beckett
Olga Beloborodova

Samuel Beckett's Geological Imagination
Mark Byron

Beckett and Sade
Jean-Michel Rabaté

Beckett's Intermedial Ecosystems: Closed Space Environments across the Stage, Prose and Media Works
Anna McMullan

Samuel Beckett and Cultural Nationalism
Shane Weller

Absorption and Theatricality: On Ghost Trio
Conor Carville

Carnivals of Ruin: Beckett, Ireland, and the Festival Form
Trish McTighe

Beckett and Stein
Georgina Nugent

Insufferable: Beckett, Gender and Sexuality
Daniela Caselli

A full series listing is available at: www.cambridge.org/eibs

Printed in the USA
CPSIA information can be obtained
at www.ICGtesting.com
LVHW011302150324
774517LV00048B/2581